Chaperito
Land Grant, Parish & Ghost Town

By
Henrietta Martinez Christmas

Thanks to the Hispanic Genealogical Research Center of New Mexico,
The Historical Society of New Mexico and
Denver GI Forum, for their support and funding.

Many thanks to my family, old friends and new friends who have taken many trips to the area of Chaperito and its environs over the last 20 years, the New Mexico State Records Center and Archives, the Archdiocese Office of Historic Artistic Patrimony and Archives and Special Collections Library for their work and help.

Photos: Any photos are courtesy of Henrietta M. Christmas unless otherwise noted.

©All Rights Reserved. 2016 Henrietta M. Christmas
LOC: 2009927278
ISBN: 978-0-9841420-1-9

Table of Contents

Preface

Part One   Chaperito

Introduction	1
Chaperito	3
Buffalo Hunting – Ciboleros	14
Sheep Ranching and Herding	17
Religion at Chaperito	19
Chaperito Schools	23
Postmasters	25
Military at Hatch's Ranch	26
1860 Census	30

Part Two   Neighboring Mission Churches & Villages

Los Valles de San Agustin	31
La Liendre	35
Los Torres, Las Lajas, Los Fuertes	38
La Concepcion	40
La Aguila	42
Cañada de Aguilar	43
Ranches & Farms of the Lower Gallinas	45
San Lorenzo	46
El Cerro de Corazon	47
Sabinoso	48
La Cinta	49
La Garita	50
La Trementina	51
Variadero	55
Cañon Largo	58
San Ramon	59
Sanchez	61
Arollo de las Conchas	62
Other Missions Served by Chaperito	64

Part Three   Other Place Names

Salitre, Trementina (La Paz)	65
Maps	69
Bibliography	72
Index	74

Preface

In originally preparing this book, I tried to address the historical aspects of the land grant of Chaperito and the immediate vicinity. As the years passed, the focus of my efforts shifted to that of migration of settlers, places seldom mentioned or known about, occupations and preservation of the history of the region. This has not been as easy a task as it was envisioned in the beginning.

In the early 1980's my maternal grandparents were extremely helpful in guiding me around as they knew many of the ranchers and people I needed to visit with. I have found that a good oral historian is worth much more than what can be found in any book or newspaper article. Their memories and instruction of how things were transported from one place to another and who did what were invaluable – research had become much more difficult when I had to do this alone. In the intervening years, land had been bought and sold and the new owners were difficult to find and often had different rules. Photographs were not allowed in some areas nor could they be used within these pages in order to comply with owners requests.

The ruins in this part of San Miguel County, New Mexico are fading mostly due to weather, theft and neglect. Very little preservation has been done to document cemeteries, preserve maps of town sites, owners of homes and various churches, post offices, stores and even corrals. Flagstone walls litter the *llano*, but no marker signifies who lived there. Archives have been scoured and little was found to document any of what I deem critical information. Villages mentioned in 1860 census are lost to us and identifying them will likely never happen as we no longer have the "old timers" to tell us where they were.

Nearly everyplace mentioned in this book is on private property, some right off county roads and others not. Anyone trying to visit them, should get written permission from the owners and a list of what pictures can be taken and how they can be used. In my enthusiasm to document these places I have not heeded my own advice and found that the desire of others were not similar to my own. The result is more work and fewer pictures that I might wish in order to tell a story.

Forty plus years later, what started out as a ride in an old Ford Truck alone with my grandparents with a lot of time to talk and ask questions has resulted in this research of the area. I will always be grateful for the time they spent with me. Today when I travel out to the *llano* they are still with me telling stories of their lives and their ancestors.

This book is for all my *antepasados* (ancestors) who forged a new life in this part of New Mexico.

Introduction

Chaperito is a ghost town that has been picked over – not even the remains of a church survive there today - the *campsanto* emerges as the only memory that this area once settled, houses have decayed and rubble fill some of the rooms. Was Chaperito"s demise a result of economic downturns, overgrazing or just fed up farmers and ranchers looking for a better way. Chaperito itself would not be considered part of the Wild West nor is it a tourist attraction so often associated with ghost towns, it is just a place that rose up and then vanished.

The early settlers came as part of a land grant -- lands which would not necessarily become those of their descendants. The first people were farmers, herders, buffalo hunters. Their move east from La Cuesta was part of a growing expansion to make a better living. Later they would become teachers, postman, freighters, drivers, soldiers and merchants.

No records exist but these men and women likely spoke some Indian languages in order to trade and keep peace with the Comanche and Kiowa. Their skills at bartering would keep them supplied during times when the Indians stole their horses, produce and at times children during times of hostility.

The other villages near Chaperito, whether they were settled earlier or later than 1846, retain a character of safety and a sense of honor with their religion. Many of them were also abandoned and cannot even be found.

Protected by nearby Ft. Hatch and then the larger town of Las Vegas the small town grew. Chaperito did not remain small for long – families grew as the Indians disappeared. Their distance from the Santa Fe Trail, trains and major roads kept them isolated. Access to new types of food, machinery and a way of life was Las Vegas, twenty-five miles away. Their more eastern neighbors remained without things such as electricity well into the 1980"s.

Many of the men and its area villages enlisted as soldiers before, during and after the Civil War. Many of these men would come home to plant their fields and do other chores instead of waiting for the superior officers to hand down new orders; the US Army called this absent without leave (AWOL). These men were used to fighting with lances, bows and arrows, rifles and whatever materials they could make -- waiting around was a waste of time. Their names in history books are sparse and many times left out. But they served to defend their country and families and so that was good enough.

By WWII, men that had left to fight in this war found out upon returning that farming or herding was not for them anymore. They wanted education and better paying jobs. Migration out of Chaperito was devastating to the small town as families left to the big cities or other states to work. Many would again never return to their homeland of Chaperito.

Now a ghost town now for many years, Chaperito no longer celebrates a feast day, no customs are maintained and the cemetery is only rarely visited. The once thriving village is barren and lifeless but for a calf's bawling, a few rundown houses or blowing wind - it has ceased to exist.

Chaperito[1]

Chaperito's place in history is largely due to eastward migration of settlers who wanted to live on the borderlands and venture out into the eastern plains or *llanos* outside of Las Vegas and Los Valles de San Agustin. A short lived settlement during the early occupation of the United States and into the 20th century, it is all but a ghost town and a memory for those older descendants of the first grantees that came to settle in this valley located on the Gallinas River. In some ways Chaperito was strategically located as a doorway to the eastern plains and its proximity to Hatch's Ranch afforded them some protection after 1860.

Santiago Martin and Jose Garcia petitioned for a grant on February 4, 1846, they were from Nuestra Señora de Guadalupe of La Cuesta (present day Villanueva) along with fifteen other individuals, although twenty-eight are listed. The grant was bounded on the north to the mouth of the Cañon, south the grant made to the persons from Puertecito (Sena), east to the point of the Conchas mesa and west to the point of the Aguilar mesa, with one half league around to serve as commons. The grant they sought had good agricultural land, plenty of water and was uninhabited. The petitioners themselves having come from the La Cuesta and are soliciting land known as Chaperito were:[2]

1. Jose Garcia
2. Santiago Martin
3. Jose Tapia
4. Jose Manuel Tapia
5. Ygnacio Aragon
6. Julian Garcia
7. Jose Antonio Tapia
8. Prudencio Tapia
9. Fernando Lucero
10. Jose Armijo
11. Juan Madrid
12. Francisco Salas
13. Jose Rael
14. Lugardo Blea
15. Lorenzo Aragon
16. Rafael Lucero
17. Jose Nieves Lucero
18. Deciderio Maes
19. Miguel Ramon Sais
20. Tomas Sais

---

[1] Julyan, Robert, *The Place Names of New Mexico*, Pg. 77. (San Miguel; settlement; 25 miles SE of Las Vegas; PO 1875 intermittently to 1957, mail to Las Vegas). Spanish, "little hat", probably a descriptive metaphor for a nearby landform. Once a major junction of routes along the Gallinas River, Chaperito now has but few residences, if not a ghost town.

[2] Spanish Archives of New Mexico, Series I, Roll 30, Surveyor General #7 "Chaperito Land Grant"

21. Gabriel Baca
22. Felipe Madrid
23. Rafael Marquez
24. Jesus Gonzales
25. Gabriel Gonzales
26. Jose Duran
27. Pablo Olgin
28. Juan Baca (frame 795)[3]

To the Justice of the Peace of Las Vegas,

We, the undersigned, Santiago Martin and Jose Garcia, residents of the precinct of Our Lady of Guadalupe of La Cuesta, for ourselves and in the name of seventeen individuals subscribed in the accompanying list, represent to you in due for: What having examined and registered the piece of land commonly called Chaperito, watered by the Gallinas River and lying in the District of Las Vegas, we find that the same is vacant and wholly uncultivated land, and is it is situated within your jurisdiction and as in you lies the power that was formerly exercised by the ayuntamientos, we ask for this public land in the name of the sacred powers of the Mexican Nation, and that we (together with as many individuals as there may be without lands of their own) be placed in possession in full conforming with the colonization law and in accordance with those laws that so imperiously enjoin the encouragement of agriculture; designating as boundaries, on the north to the mouth of the Cañon, on the south the grant made to the persons from Puertecito and which land was given them in possession in your district last year, on the east the point of the Conchas mesa to the further side thereof, and on the west the point of the Aguilar mesa, all of which we pray for without injury to any third party.

Therefore, we humbly pray that you be pleased to consider us before you, awaiting with all deference the superior orders of His Honor the Prefect of the First Municipality, should he deem it necessary to given them in order to strengthen your action, for we believe the case to be one of strict justice, which is what we seek.
Note: We stand obligated to attach the proper revenue stamp.
Our Lady of Guadalupe of La Cuesta, February 4, 1846
Signed: Santiago Martin (cross)
Jose Garcia (cross)[4]

Juan de Dios Maes, Justice of the Peace of Las Vegas signed on February 4, 1846 at Las Vegas attesting to the above information and making his claim that he has jurisdiction.

On March 10, 1846, the Republic of Mexico gave them title to the lands, noted was one half league around it to serve as commons for the population.   The grant was finalized and signed by Jose Francisco Baca y Terrus, Justice of the Peace of the 3rd

---

[3] Spanish Archives of New Mexico, Series I, SG #7, Frame 795. List of Chaperito grantees.
[4] Spanish Archives of New Mexico, Series I, SG #7, Frames 814, 815

Demarcation of El Bado. Tomas Ortiz, named the individuals and the land was to be used to sow seed and the half league around about used as pasture land.

These grantees were part of a generation of people whose ancestors had done this before, first settling in San Miguel del Bado, later moving into Las Vegas, La Cuesta and Anton Chico. Knowing what they knew to be a must, for any type of settlement was water, land and then fortification. Many of these early settlements started out with the grazing of sheep, building houses or plazas for safety and then moving their families when things were secure -- Chaperito was no different. Chaperito had many acequias that ran up and down the Gallinas River for farming purposes; many of these were likely built when they first moved into the area. They found grazeable land, water and a place to live safely; settling here was just another notch on the map and one step further down the road on the borderlands of New Mexico.

Their histories and futures intertwined, not only in the coming decade of 1850 and into the next century, but also by marrying into each other's families and venturing together to settle further from the capital of Santa Fe.

The U. S. invaded New Mexico in 1848 and now Chaperito was under a different sovereignty. By 1885, land grants in New Mexico were being sought by anyone who could make a claim. Legal transfer of property, testimonies and surveyor general employees all had a hand in defining what would become and who would own specific land grants.

Chaperito"s claim began when the Antonio Ortiz Grant began encroaching on the Chaperito Grant and legal means were instituted to determine who was there first. The Antonio Ortiz Grant had already been confirmed and Chaperito would not win this battle. On July 14, 1888, interviews began with elder residents who had lived in the area since birth or before. Present were George N. Julian, U.S. Surveyor General for the Territory of New Mexico, Judge Francis Downs, attorney for the Chaperito claimants and Will M. Tipton, translator of the Surveyor General's Office, who acted as interpreter.

The first interview was conducted with Graviel Gonzales who was 68 years old and he was born around 1820 and claimed he lived at Chaperito since about 1844 and still resides there. He made mention that for the exception of one occasion when all the Chaperito people left on account of the Indians, but did return the same year and took possession again. He recalled the petition for the land was made by *don* Juan de Dios Maes from Las Vegas and was the Justice at the time. He continued to tell them that he had purchased the land from Jesus Gonzales, his brother. Graviel Gonzales later tells them that there must be more than a hundred now living at Chaperito in three plazas and that people from Los Torres claimed land under this grant.

Simon Garcia was next; he was 48 years old and had lived there since it was settled. He was the son of Jose Garcia who was a grantee and had sold it to Juan de la Cruz Lucero. Simon Garcia claimed his father lived there from the time it was settled until he moved to La Cuesta in 1868. Asked about the distance to Las Vegas, Garcia stated it was twenty-five miles. He claimed there was some conflict with ownership, replying that in 1877 or 1878 that some notices had been put up in Chaperito by Chapman, but was not certain if Catron and Elkins had also signed them ordering Chaperito to not cut timber.

Teodosio Salas stated he was 56 years old and that he had a house and land in Chaperito. He recalled the place known as Chaperito from around 1845; his grandfather had sheep and land which he took care of. His father was Francisco Salas and was still alive and his grandfather, who had the sheep, was Juan Andres Garcia, who had purchased the land from a widow of Jose Manuel Tapia who was killed by Indians; Teodosio Salas now owning the land. Salas claimed they had moved the whole family in 1855. His response to the distance to Las Vegas was thirty miles by another road and twenty-five by horseback. He said that in 1877 notices were put up in Chaperito prohibiting them from cultivating land, cutting timber or making any kind of improvements; not happy they put a petition to Congress about the matter through *don* Trinidad Romero. Salas was asked about the roads to Fort Bascom by the *Ojitos de la Conchas* -- he knew them, but when asked about roads in 1845 and 1846 he said there were none, just *llano*. He said an old road had been made by the buffalo hunters which he knew long ago, about 1850, then about 1863-1864 he went over this road with many other men with 100 wagons, traveling to the States and opening the old road up more. Teodosio Salas's grandfather had lived at La Cuesta prior to him moving here and people would travel on a road from here to there (what would now be the same road to Fort Bascom). Memory serving him well, he continued to state that they traveled to La Cuesta with pack mules around 1850, but the newer road to the Fort was later in 1863 or "64.

Francisco E. Robledo was nearly 45 years and lived at Chaperito since April 1875 having purchased the land. He was aware with the conflict of the Antonio Ortiz Grant; Chapman, Elkins and Catron all putting up notices and the Surveyor General's involvement. In 1881, he took a Mr. Campbell, a surveyor, with him to show the eastern line of the Ortiz Grant in order to find out whether there might be some government land that between the Ortiz and Pino (Preston Beck) Grants. In 1885 a Mr. White had paid him to show where the north east line of the Ortiz grant was situated. When asked about the roads he claimed that the road to Fort Bascom was also known as the Red River road. Asked about the Rincon de los Chupaines and the mesa of the Chupaines and the Ojito of los Chupaines, Robledo stated they are three different places. These boundaries were part of the Antonio Ortiz Grant and Chupaines which had a road which the old men used for buffalo hunting and was first opened in that part of this country. Discussing the boundaries, he stated that the cerro de Laureno and some call it Rincon and or cañada de Laureno, but there is no cañon, being north of Chaperito. The location of the mesitas de las Conchas is about three miles east of the Mesa de los Carros, west of the Arroyo de las Conchas. He knew that Chaperito was situated on the Gallinas River, the Arroyo de las Conchas and the Cañada de Aguilar were all within boundaries of the Chaperito Grant. Other settlements within the Chaperito Grant were Los Torres, La Aguila, Las Conchas, El Aguilar, Las Lajas, and he believed La Liendre. Robledo responded when asked about a post office and church that both existed at Chaperito and claimed that the town was on the east side of the Gallinas River.

Jose Benito Baca, was 57 years old and lived at Chaperito having lived there since November 1859. He owned land by purchase and was a resident of Santa Fe prior to that. He stated boundaries, the road and the Antonio Ortiz Grant just as the others had.

Placido Apodaca, was 52 years old and lived at Chaperito since 1848, his father having been a grantee, land that he now owns. Like the others he stated boundaries, cerro de Laureno, Las Conchas, Fort Bascom and the conflict with the Antonio Ortiz Grant.

Manuel Montoya y Martinez was 58 years, a resident and worked at Chaperito since 1847 making dams. He recounted that the Indians had run them off, but they returned in the spring of 1849. Manuel's grandfather, Santiago Martinez, was one of the petitioners. Manuel's father having died, he lived with his grandfather, Santiago, who gave him 50 varas of land before he died. Asked about the Indian raids, he stated that many settlers were killed in the vicinity of Chaperito. Some were wounded, others carried off as captives, soldiers were also killed. His recollection of the roads going by Chupaines was that people used it from El Bado and went out after buffaloes. Further boundaries were restated, the cañada and Rincon de Laureno being to the north of Chaperito.

**Riverbank in Chaperito, NM, photo by: Fristz Broeske,
Courtesy Palace of the Governors (MNM/DCA) Negative no. 119861**

A listing of the current residents petitioning for this matter to be resolved included the following schedule of the names of the settlers, now residing on the "Chaperito Grant" of land in San Miguel County, New Mexico; and claiming thereto, 1888.

1. Jose Apodaca
2. Lucrecio Lucero
3. Jose E. Lucero
4. Telesfor Lucero
5. Placido Apodaca
6. Francisco E. Robeldo
7. Apolonio Duran
8. Candelario Gallegos
9. Jose Gallegos
10. Desiderio Apodaca
11. Felix Garcia
12. Encarnacion de Herrera
13. Salbador Martin
14. Jose Lovato
15. Rafael Garcia y Urioste
16. Francisco Garcia y Gonzales
17. Esquipula Lopez
18. Tiburcio Garcia
19. Santiago Gonzales
20. Jose Miguel Archuleta
21. Esquipula Gallegos
22. Ricardo Gallegos
23. Nicolas Martines
24. Gabriel Martines
25. Pedro Aragon
26. Nicolas Mestas
27. Trinidad Apodaca
28. Ygnazio Gonzales
29. Gabriel Gonzales
30. Tomas Gallegos
31. Francisco Gallegos
32. Juan Apodaca
33. Jose Flores
34. Juan Flores
35. Ponsio Garsilla
36. Esperidon Garduño
37. Jesus Martines
38. Luis Duran
39. Esteban Aragon
40. Esteban Gallegos
41. Rafael Garsia y Carillo
42. Leonides Flores
43. Jose de la Crus Apodaca
44. Gregorio Garduño
45. Pablo Jaramillo
46. Felis Lusero
47. Antonio Jaramillo
48. Luis Jaramillo
49. Ventura Jaramillo
50. Juan Jesus Tapia
51. Manuel Montoya
52. Francisco Anallo
53. Tomas Velasquez
54. Juan Sena
55. Encarnacion Valdez
56. Francisco Baros
57. Manuel Flores y Esquibel (frame 825)
58. Sencion Garcia
59. Antonio Encinias
60. Simon Butieres
61. Antonio Salazar
62. Atanacio Duran
63. Antonio Alarcon
64. Matias Gonzales
65. Pablo Rivera
66. Guadalupe Tapia
67. Miguel Garcia
68. Remejio Angel
69. Jesus Gomez
70. Pablo Gomez
71. Lucrecio Gomez
72. Jose Garcia y Carrillo
73. Eusebio Lucero
74. Antonio Maria Lucero
75. Juan Mora
76. Juan Climaco Lucero
77. Juan de la Cruz Lucero
78. Luis Baca
79. Jose Domingo Butierres

80. Jose Gregorio Rivera
81. Manuel Flores 1°
82. Daniel Flores
83. Rafael Gonzales y Esquibel
84. Juan Gonzales y Sena
85. Simon Gonzales
86. Filomeno Maestas
87. Jose Romulo Lucero
88. Placido Lucero
89. Julio Chavez
90. Marcos Duran
91. Ysidro Tafoya
92. Dimas Chavez
93. Atanacio Garcia
94. Juan Jose Gallegos
95. Francisco Gonzales y Apodaca
96. Lorenzo Garcia
97. Cruz Gallegos
98. Sefirino de Herrera
99. Higinio Lucero
100. Andres Garcia
101. Francisco Lucero
102. Jose Lucero
103. Felipe M. Lucero
104. Eligio Ortega
105. Tomas Pacheco
106. Marcos Garsilla
107. Dolores Lucero
108. Pedro Ribera
109. Jose Lion Garsilla
110. Carmen Chavez
111. Santos Vigil
112. Jose Ynes Sena
113. Teodoro Sandobal
114. Manuel Apodaca
115. Nasario Garcia
116. Teodoro Garcia
117. Jose Romero
118. Ramon Salas
119. Ynes Pinon (frame 826)
120. Antonio Sena
121. Pedro Lucero
122. Abran Sandoval
123. Pablo Ortega
124. Antonio Baros
125. Benigno Montoya
126. Silverio Archuleta
127. Jose Madril
128. Hilario Duran
129. Tiodoso Salas
130. Canuto Lucero
131. Jose Ynosencio Lucero
132. Labrado Apodaca
133. Juliana Garcia
134. Josefa Madril
135. Jose Maria Baros
136. Jesus Gallegos
137. Camilo Gallegos
138. Merejildo Gallegos
139. Francisco Gallegos
140. Onofre Gallegos
141. Emilio Flores
142. Higinio Sena
143. Maria Rita Mares
144. Francisco Sena
145. Gregorio Flores
146. Patricio Montaño
147. Jose de Jesus Duran
148. Jose Benito Baca
149. Amado Baca
150. Miguel Baca
151. Ramon Baca
152. Luis S. Montaño
153. Antonio A. Romero
154. Pablo Gonsales
155. Mariano Archuleta
156. Carmel Martino
157. Jose Marilla Apodaca
158. Albino Apodaca
159. Juan Martines
160. Jose de la Cruz Gonsales
161. Victoriano Lucero
162. Juan A. Arguello
163. Juan Pedro Montaño
164. Sencion Arguello
165. Jose de los Relles Balerde
166. Marselino Baros
167. Antonio D. Ruibal
168. Gerorgo Blea
169. Leonordo Gonsales
170. Juan de Martines
171. Francisco Ruibal

172. Neposeno Gonsales	178. Juan Garcia
173. Rafael Mendosa	179. Manuel Balverde
174. Juan Rael	180. Domingo Aragon
175. Juan Francisco Blea	181. Juan Jose Duran
176. Anacleto Martinez	182. Bibion Duran
177. Jose Guadalupe Mtz	

Documents produced at the request of the U.S. Government show named individuals, land size and neighbors bordered. These land titles are all dated between March 6, 1846 and June 23, 1855, at Las Vegas or at Los Valles de San Agustin and signed by Juan de Dios Maes, Justice. On these records, not all of them are petitioners nor heirs; by this time the land had been sold off to someone else.

In this demarcation of Nuestra Señora de los Dolores, Las Vegas, 20th March 1846, before Juan de Dios Maese, Justice of the Peace of the 3rd Demarcation of which was once San Miguel del Bado... named Chaperito on the Gallinas River, named for the Patron Saint of San Ysidro. Lands were registered to the following with noted boundaries:

1. **Graviel Gonzales**, (wife, Juana Sena), 150 varas, bordered to the north by Jesus Gonzales, south the lands of Jose Garduño, east the river and west *la loma* (hill).
2. **Jesus Gonzales**, (Gertrudis Montaño), 250 varas, bordered to the north lands of Jose Miguel Apodaca, south the lands of Graviel Gonzales, east the river and west *la loma.*
3. **Jose Garcia**, (Francisca Urioste), 50 varas, bordered to the north by Jose Tapia, south the river, east the acequia madre and west the river.
4. **Miguel Garcia**,[5] (Maria Antonia Gonzales), 400 varas, bordered to the north by Francisco Olguin, south the curve of the river, east *la loma* and west the river.
5. **Francisco Olguin**, (Lorenza Varela), 250 varas, bordered to the north by Ramon Duran, the south the lands of Miguel Garcia, east *la loma*, and west the river.
6. **Jose Tapia**, (Guadalupe Sanchez), 100 varas of cultivated land, bordered to the north by Fernando Lucero, south the lands of Jose Garcia, east the acequia madre and west the river.
7. **Fernando Lucero**, (Agapita Tapia), 100 varas, bordered to the north the lands of Jose Manuel Tapia, the south land of Jose Tapia, east the acequia madre and west the river.
8. **Jose Lucero,** (Maria Luciana Flores), 100 varas, bordered to the north by Jose Manuel Tapia, south the land of Jose Tapia, east the acequia madre and west the river.
9. **Pedro Maldonado,**[6] 100 varas, bordered on the east by lands of Miguel Montaño, west the lands *de lo Torre*, south the common lands, north the lands

---

[5] At times some records indicate he is Rafael, likely in error of the scribe.

of Jose de la Cruz and Miguel Muñiz. Another document shows land sale from Jose Maria Sanchez and his wife, Esquipula Lujan to Gregorio Montaño and Jose Felipe Montaño.

10. **Jose de la Cruz Casias**, (Maria Dolores Marquez), 1050 varas, bordered to the west land of Juan Rael, east lands of Jose Miguel Muñiz, north the common lands and south the mesa of Aguilar.
11. **Nicolas Martines**, (Maria Feliciana Gonzales), 112 varas, bordered to the north by lands of Francisco Olgin, south land of Francisco Herrera, east the common lands and west the river.
12. **Santiago Gonzales**, (Maria Manuela), 200 varas, bordered to the north by lands of Ygnacio Aragon, south Roque Anaya, west the river and east the common lands.
13. **Juan Ysidro Duran**, (Faustina Gonzales), 350 varas, bordered to the north by lands of Manuel Apodaca, to the south land of Ricardo Gallegos, east the river and west the common lands.
14. **Nicolas Mestas**, (Maria de la Luz Garcia), 112 varas, bordered north by the lands of Francisco Herrera, south the lands of Ygnacio Aragon, east the common land and west the river.
15. **Francisco Herrera**, 100 varas, bordered to the north by lands of Nicolas Martinez, south Nicolas Mestas, west the river and east *las lomas*.
16. **Jose Felipe Madril**, (Encarnacion Sandoval), 150 varas, bordered to the north by land of Ygnacio Aragon, south land of Pedro Gallegos, west the river and east the common lands.
17. **Juan Acencion Lopes**, 800 varas, bordered to the north by the river, south *las lomas* of the common lands, west lands of Pedro Gallegos and east *el llano*.
18. **Jose Miguel/Manuel Apodaca**, (Juana Moya), 250 varas, bordered north by the river, south the lands of Jesus Gonzales, east the river and west *la loma*.

The settlers kept their lands after the investigation, proving they had legally deeded property. They had lived there continuously since they grant was given to them and produced deeds and verbal witnesses to make their claims. Over the years, they would inherit, buy and eventually sell all the land. Chaperito became a ghost town when the Post Office closed down in 1957.

---

[6] Possibly was a Montaño as the Maldonado families sometimes used the names interchangeably. The family of Manuel Montaño is living at Los Torres in 1860 with $150 value of real estate.

Lands at Chaperito
Not to scale

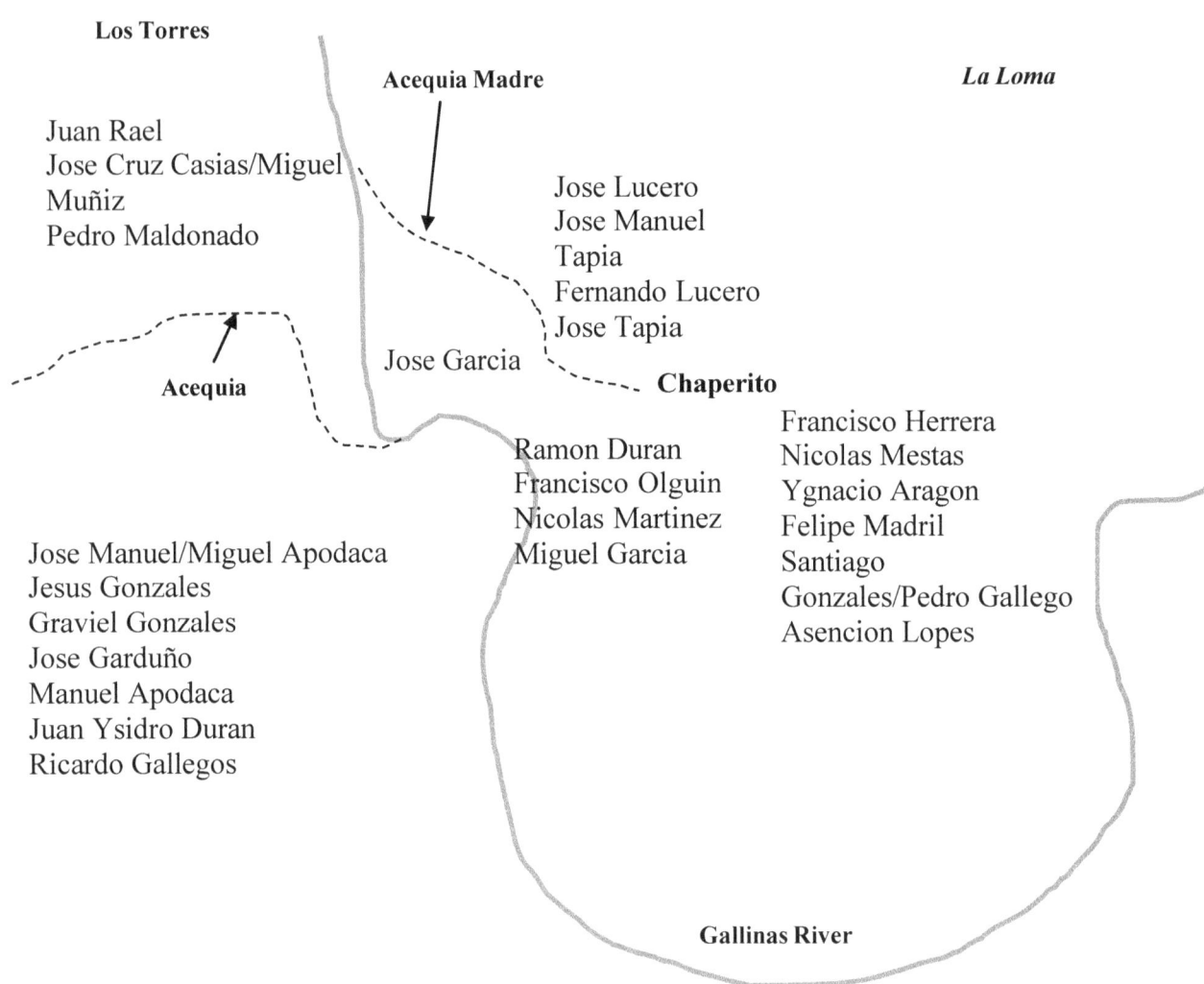

Lands owned based on their testimony.

By 1860, Chaperito had become a thriving small town with a population of 436 individuals. Their closest neighbors were noted as the Borough of Los Torres, with some of the original land grantees living here and not at Chaperito, Las Lajas followed having several individuals. Other suburbs to Chaperito were Cañada de Aguilar, El Aguila, Los Luceros, Rancho del Rio de las Conchas, San Agustin and San Antonio (La Liendre). The area continued to grow each subsequent decade and migration eastward went as far as Sabinoso, Trementina and areas near now Conchas Dam.

Chaperito began to wind down after WWII and by 1957 they no longer had a post office; men returning from the war wanted to make a living in the city, receive college education; moving north to Colorado or west to California. The vastness of what Chaperito became was evidenced by the parish church and the many mission churches it served. Although settlers did keep title to their lands, Chaperito was never recognized as a "true" land grant as was the Antonio Ortiz which lies over the area. They land owners did keep their lands and continued to buy and sell well into the mid 1900"s. The area we know as Chaperito is now singly owned and is a large ranch in that part of San Miguel County.

Buffalo Hunting – *Ciboleros*

The majority of the hunting parties known as *ciboleros* went to an area known as the *llano estacado*, in eastern New Mexico and into west Texas when the first Spaniards came in 1542; although some hunting parties went to the eastern plains of Colorado. The New Mexico plains stretching into Texas provided tall grass for the buffalo herds during their southern migration. The plant life on the *llano* provided some food for the hunters, poles (used to hang the meat) and wood for campfires.[7] By 1870 the buffalo were mostly confined to the south Cimarron and Canadian rivers with some trails running out of Ft. Sumner eastward. The *puertas* or doors into the plains were well known by the hunters and were all located by Chaperito and La Aguila. Hunters from these Chaperito villages all hunted annually.

It took many months to prepare for a hunt. Ten-foot long lances were tipped with 18-inch razor sharp iron blades; bows and arrows were made, and knives for skinning and cutting the meat were sharpened. Plus, the party gathered foodstuffs and other supplies for the trip. After all of the preparations, the skilled *ciboleros* along with their lances, fast horses and maybe some rifles, set out on the hunt.

Hunters wore buckskin clothing and moccasins. In winter they wore tied skin leggings and a large brimmed hat. Upon their shoulders hung their *carcage* or quiver of bows and arrows and their lances were strapped to the pommel of the saddle. Their rifles (if they had them) were suspended in like manner on the other side. If a hunter used a rifle, he would load it with powder and shot while galloping on his horse, lean down to hit the butt of the rifle on the ground to settle the shot and then shoot. No time was wasted since rushing into a buffalo herd was extremely dangerous and the hunter had to kill as many buffalo as quickly as he could.[8]

Hunting parties typically consisted of 200 or more people. Sometimes women and children came along to help with the less dangerous jobs. Hunting parties were led by a *mayordomo* who had full control of the party. Other members of the party had their own roles including:
- *el cazador*, the lancer
- el *sigador*, would follow closely and slit the throats of the buffalo
- *el carrero*, drove the carts
- *el dueno*, cart owner
- *el guisandero*, meat preservers
- *el agregado*, packed and transported the meat back home.

The *cazador* would drive the lance right behind the buffalo's shoulder blade, pull it out and continue on to the next buffalo. The *sigador* followed close behind, and so on.

---

[7] Morris, John Miller; *El Llano Estacado: Exploration and Imagination of the High Plains of Texas and New Mexico 1536-1860* (Texas state Historical Association, 1997) 80, 157.
[8] Gregg, Josiah, *Commerce of the Prairies* (University of Oklahoma Press) 63.

Once the buffalo was dead, the *carrero* pulled the wagon close to the buffalo and it was skinned on the ground. The *guisandero* began work immediately, slicing the meat into long thin strips. Thin strips of buffalo hide were brought along and used like clotheslines to hang the meat for drying. Since the hunt would last up to a month or longer, the meat had plenty of time to cure. Finally, party members rolled up the strips of meat or pushed it into sacks and stomped it down for transporting.

Upon returning to the village, the meat, hides, bones and other parts were divided among those that participated in the hunt. The annual hunts and the buffalo products they acquired helped the villagers to supplement their other foodstuffs throughout the winter and early spring. Almost every part of the buffalo was used. Salted buffalo tongues were sold as a delicacy in Mexico City. The horns were used for utensils, neck hair for stuffing mattresses and fat was made into tallow, which was used for cooking and candle making.

The *indita* (ballad) of Manuel Maes relates his buffalo hunting accident of 1873. As he was chasing a buffalo his horse stumbled and his lance pierced him. As he lay dying, he recalled a premonition of death, his mother held him while he died and the bells tolled. Manuel Maes was from Chaperito.

English Translation of the Ballad of Manuel Maes

I ask for your attention folks
I ask it for the last time.
Good-by beloved *compadres*
Of the late Manuel Maes
To this world I say farewell
In this year of seventy-three.

On Saturday in the morning
I had knowledge of my death
The tolling of the bells I heard
And these plainly told me
That my mother Donaciana
In her arms was holding me.

Sunday early in the day
My final hour I knew
About three in the afternoon
My soul left my body
In the arms of a *compadre*
Who not even "Jesus" invoked.

My cousin Mauricio Tapia
Was the first one to reach
The spot where I was lying

He took me in his arms
Saying: Manuelito
What has happened to you?

Oh my sorrel colored horse
That you should have been my death
I found that I was tired
And lost my hold on my lance
And do the prairie sod is drenched
With my blood you dyed it.

Of all the horses we brought
My sorrel is the swiftest
Yet this misfortune befell me
A prairie dog hole threw him
I lost my lance in the fall
It pierced my body thru and thru.

And that famed black horse
I was left with the desire
Of seeing myself on your back
I had thought of hunting buffalo
But my luck turned against me
And I see I had planned wrong.

On the Colorado River
I have eaten watermelons
Surrounded by my brothers
Who were in my company
Now my body will be buried
In their soil like a seed.

Near the shores of a lake
Where they are going to bury me
Like a prickly pear plant without its fruit
Youth! Here you'll remain.

Cañon del Agua to all well known
You'll be my resting place
And of my beloved parents
I wish their blessing
I hope they will command
That my soul should have absolution.

My heart has warned me
That death was imminent
On this Staked Plain
I will leave my skeleton.

Maria Ramona Maes
Goodbye beloved sister
For the last time goodbye
My time for leaving has come
This year of "73.

Goodbye Dominguito Maes
Very young, I leave you
Goodbye Maria Desideria
Your brother is leaving you
You will never see him again
Entering his humble *jacal*.

Goodbye Lauriano peak
Which from my house can be seen
Goodbye Mother Donaciana
And my father Juan de Dios Maes
To this world I say farewell
In this year of seventy-three.

Where these news reach
Throughout New Mexico
Will they not regret
The death of such a gentleman?
Day and night they will weep
More so when they see my hat.

He who composed this *Indita*
A very humble and blundering youth
Excuse me if I make mistakes
If I leave out important facts
I will make my name known.
I am Cecilio Roybal
To sing this *Indita*
It is necessary to pray
A sudarium for the deceased
Of whom I have spoken;
May God free him from torment
And take him home to rest.

Fin (The End)

by Lorin W. Brown[9]

---

[9] Fray Angelico Chavez Library. History Files.

Sheep Ranching and Herding

Sheepherders known as *pastores* were prominent in this part of San Miguel County. Large owners of sheep along with their own small herds were grazed in the grasslands from La Cuesta out to Trementina. Dry rock fences along the Gallinas River were built to pen them in and trails leading down to water were made by these herders. *tinajas,* watering holes, could be found in arroyos up and down the pastures. Prior to 1846, large herds of sheep were driven south on the *camino real* into Mexico. In 1844, 52,000 sheep were taken south.

After the Treaty of Guadalupe, this type of commerce with Mexico dried up. *Pastores* still had work to do, but their own sheep were of primary concern. Young men at the ages of seven and up would herd sheep during the day and as they got older would be sent out to the Canadian River, Trementina Creek and as far away as the Rio Puerco to herd sheep for months. Most herders had dogs to accompany them and help with keeping herds under control. With large herds the herders generally lived with the sheep and may or may not have had a horse or a burro.

Sheep in the *llano* have many predators, the coyote being the worst. Other animals, foxes, large birds and mountain lions all prey on them. Lambs were more susceptible to predators and generally were kept more confined until they grew a bit. The herder had plenty of work to do keeping his herds safe.

Like buffalo hunting, sheep herding had a *mayordomo* or the rancher and overseers who were in charge of the herders. The sheep camps were made in locations that were safe from the weather, open to the *llano* and easy to access. Some men worked sheep under the *partido* system and did this for a life time. Others owned their own and employed herders depending on the size of their herd.

Lambing season was in the spring and everyone in the household took part along with the herders. Small lambs sometimes needed help and children could help feed them. If the weather changed, fires had to be built or taken to large barns or penned areas. When ewes who didn't want their lambs had to be hand fed or fostered to another ewe, which at times wouldn't work. Weaning the lambs from their mothers was another huge undertaking as they would need to be separated until the both of them could live without the other.

Tresquiladores,[10] sheep shearers, would come in and shear sheep once a year in the summer. Using *tijeras de tresquilar,* wool scissors, they could shear many sheep in one day. The wool would be placed in huge gunny sacks and piled high in wagons and transported to Las Vegas to be transported via rail. Professional shearers would travel from ranch to ranch and participate in this huge event.

---

[10] Cobos, Ruben. *"A Dictionary of New Mexico & Southern Colorado Spanish,"* pg. 230. Esquilador is the correct term.

Sheep were marked on the ear, *señalaban*, in order to keep owners from mixing their animals. Clipping or cutting certain areas or shapes of their ears, known as notching, was used to signify ownership. Castrating and sometimes clipping their tails would all be done at the same time. *Carneros*, rams, *borregas*, ewes, and *borregitos*, lambs all went through parts of this process.

Ranchers had to register their brands for sheep separate than from cattle and horses as the latter are generally branded.

Some Registered sheep brands:

Florencio Arellanes from La Concepcion, October 26, 1891.

Isidro Tafoya, El Aguila, October 31, 1892.

Jose E. Apodaca, La Aguila, January 2, 1896.

Ramon Martinez, from Sabinoso, September 24, 1898.

Dolores Gallegos, from Chaperito, November 3, 1898.

Santiago Blea, from Trementina, February 23, 1899.[11]

Sheep were herded to the nearest railroads either in Las Vegas, Wagon Mound or Newkirk. Instead of going through a weaning process they would just separate them when it was time to sell.

The life of a sheep herder could be lonely, but if not for them many families would not have had food to eat or money to purchase other items. Like buffalo hunting, the life of a *pastor* is gone; large herds no longer roam the *llano* and many ranchers turned to cattle in order to make a living.

---

[11] San Miguel County Brand Books, New Mexico State Records Center and Archives, #15367.

Religion at Chaperito

Chapel under Anton Chico and the Beginnings of the Parish of Chaperito. A chapel under the jurisdiction of Anton Chico was first noted in 1859,[12] although the first baptism is recorded August 30, 1857 for Luis Trujeque. To discuss Chaperito, one needs to understand the church at Anton Chico also. The Parish of San Jose was not official until 1857; up until that time it had been attended by San Miguel del Bado. In 1857 it fell under the Las Vegas Parish and in 1858 it was named Asuncion de Nuestra Señora. By 1859, Rev. J. B. Fayet was head of the parish at Anton Chico and the missions which fell under that jurisdiction were Chaperito and Los Valles. The new church of San Jose began construction in 1860 and appears to have been completed by 1865; but noted as a parish in 1857. The San Jose church was built in the baroque style; records start in 1857 and the majority of them are for Chaperito, Los Valles de San Agustin and San Antonio (La Liendre). This parish would later be in a different county and serve a different, much smaller community.

Chaperito's cemetery, house, corral and placita was deeded to the church on June 3, 1878. The *camposanto* was recorded from Lorenzo Valdez to J. B. Lamy on November 7, 1894. The description that the cemetery was located to the north and east of the said plaza of Chaperito; with its lines to the north, the rights of the common land, to the south fifteen yards, to the west the road to Las Conchas and east the *fabrica* (church) forty yards.[13] Also signing was Manuel Montoya, Francisco Lusero and Abraham Martines.

History: The Catholic Almanac, first notes in 1859 that the chapel of Chaperito was serviced by the parish Priest of Anton Chico. From 1859-1871, the chapel fell under that jurisdiction. By 1872, noted in the Catholic Almanac, the priest Rev. L. Bourdier was attending the Chaperito Church known then as San Antonio Parish (La Liendre). For the next couple of years, the church was still being attended by Anton Chico. In 1876, the church was given the privilege of being a parish; known then as San Antonio Parish. In 1877, Rev. N. Galon served the parish and Chaperito began servicing their mission churches. For the next 70 years some would come and go as part of that parish; a few of which are still being used today. Why Chaperito was chosen over Los Valles de San Agustin or La Liendre as the parish seat is unknown.

The church structure itself is vernacular in style as it is most apparent that the native populations produced their own shelter based on traditions of using locally available materials. In the case of Chaperito and its" missions, this would be flagstone, adobe, *latillas* and a corrugated roof. The buildings are generally long and narrow and the exterior is non-ornamented or plain.

The Patron changes from San Antonio to San Ysidro el Labrador beginning in 1892, as noted in the Catholic Directory. The name change may have been a perpetual error from 1876.

---

[12] Catholic Almanac, 1859, "Anton Chico, Rev. J. B. Fayet, who attends Los Valles and El Chaperito".
[13] San Miguel County Clerk's Office, Deed Book, Book 44, pg. 163.

Records for the church start in 1876 for baptisms and marriages; indexes in 1886; and death indexes shown are 1885-1908. These records would be available from the Family History Libraries. The Archdiocese of Santa Fe, holds the records for the years beginning in 1876 for Baptisms and Marriages. The book covers are a paper product and two of the volumes have been rebound. The first baptism noted in the sacramental book of Anton Chico was for Luis Trujeque on August 30, 1857, son of Jose Miguel Trujeque and Maria Guadalupe Gonzales.

Chaperito is also known to have a Presbyterian Missionary named Miss Alice Blake teach school in 1900. Folks from Los Valles de San Agustin and El Aguila had converted in the late 1880"s and their need for spiritual guidance and education was met with missionaries stationed around these areas.

Mission Churches: In 1878 the chapels attended by Chaperito were Los Valles, La Liendre, and San Lorenzo. The chapels of Las Colonias and Puerto de Luna were attended out of Anton Chico. In 1876, the Anton Chico priest resided over both Anton Chico and Chaperito Parishes. From the Catholic Directories it appears that some overlap of recording sacramental records may have occurred. The Catholic Directory notes that in 1888 several settlements and ranches are scattered along the Canadian River and are attended by Chaperito.

Church near Chaperito, NM, P h o t o by: Fritz Broeske
Courtesy Palace of the Governors, Negative No. 119863

Chaperito *Camposanto*:

Pedro Alcon b. April 29 1879 d. February 7 1883
Casimiro Apodaca February 11 1939, 35 years
Josefa Apodaca December 30 1908
Isavel Apodaca
Etiminio Apodaca 1914
Leopoldo Apodaca 1941
Manuelita Apodaca March 5 1895
Rosa Aragon September 21 1908
Jose Baca April 18 1927
Luis Baca July 27 1914
Evaristo Crespin 29 March
Dominika Duran February 6, 1909, 2 ½ years
Enrique Duran November 5 1919, 30 years
Felipa Duran May 15 1898
Hilario Duran June 7 1919, 70 years
Paulita Ensina
Andres Gallegos September 26 1903
Eusebio Gallegos   September 17 1932
Ines Gallegos April 19 1916
Nicolas Gallegos
Paz A. Gallego November 30 1936, 60 years
Antonio Garamillo
Carmelita Garcia September 25 19___
Epimenia Garcia 1919
Antonia____ & Fidel Gomez January 1 1921
M. Crus Gonsales February 27 1892
Josefa de Herrera June 1896
Lus Herrera April 14 1911
Efre Lucero October 10 1903
Esteban Lucero December 20 1898 – June 10 1927
Felis Lucero March 25 "33 (1922 at top)
Fidencio Lucero July 28 1929, age 51
Higinio Lucero March 25 1986, 88 years
Juan de Dios Lucero b. 1869 d. February 14 1932
Julianita Lucero July 1899
(female) Martinez September 23 1894
Carlota Martinez
Erinea Martinez 15_____1913, 59 years
Francisco Martinez Sergt. NM Cav Co. 1
Magdalena Martinez February 11 1904
Manuelita Montoya 1909 d. March 14 1934; wife of Livorio Montoya
____Mestas October 5 1919
Max Mora b. July 1871
Juanita O. April 5 1919

Vidal Olguin February 1 1851, 76 years
Jose L. Ortega August 10 1925 d. December 27, 2007; Cpl US Army
Mary Ann Ortega b. October 10 "58 d. November _
Juanita Rivera b. June 24 "01 d. April 11 "47; second stone Juanita R. Lucero
Pedro Rivera 1929
Tersita Salas March 9 1911
Tomacita Salas November 7 1929
Josefita G. de Sena b. July 1879 d. July 20 1903
Manuelita Sena 189__
Maria A. Susna Tapia
Maria Tr_____April 3 190_
Alfredo Juan Urioste August 1931 – August 1932
Teresa____melico b. August 6 1908 d. January 13 1959

Priests who served at Chaperito-

1871 **Rev. Louis Bourdier**

1877 **Rev. N. Galon** (Juan Baptiste); installed as first Pastor of Chaperito until 1885, including Texas missions, of Atascosa, Trujillo, Ojo de San Juan, Las Salinas, Mobeetie and New Mexico missions of Revuelto, San Lorenzo, San Rafael and Cuervo.

1886 **Rev. Joseph Gourcy**, includes Las Conchas, Alamogordo, Los Torres, Rio Colorado.

1890 **Rev. Paul Anet Gilberton**

1893 **Rev. Juan Baptiste Carpentier**

1897 **Rev. Joseph Claudius Balland**; repaired church and rectory. Organized Children of May and Carmel Society, 1897.

1889 **Rev. John George Splinters**; Records at Springer include Rio Colorado, El Variadero, La Cinta, Cañon Largo, Trementina and Ft. Bascom.

1907 **Rev. Pierre Plantard**; unable to cope with mission conditions he returned to France.

1914 **Rev. Peter Kueppers**

1921 **Rev. Leon Delavelle**

1923 **Rev. Maxime Mayeux**

Chaperito Schools

Chaperito School. Photo Courtesy of the Citizen"s Committee for Historic Preservation, #1035, circa 1925

Early schoolrooms usually consisted on mother's teaching their children basic math and reading when they were younger. As villages grew many would hire a teacher and each family would pitch in for the salary. As Chaperito grew and school districts developed, they had a school and a paid teacher.

The San Miguel County Schools recognized the Chaperito School starting in 1879 with records accounting for District 10 and the teacher was F. de Frouville; the same years Los Jacales, La Liendre, San Lorenzo and Sabinoso all were paying teachers about $90 for salary and house rent.

Information taken from the Superintendent Papers for San Miguel County.[14]
September 3, 1879-
Pct. 6 Los Jacales
Pct. 10 Chaperito, teacher was F. de Frouville[15]

September 25, 1879-

---

[14] San Miguel County, New Mexico, *School Superintendent Papers*. New Mexico State Records Center and Archives, Santa Fe, NM. Serial #15372 (1879-1905)
[15] Ancestry.com. He died on August 13, 1894 and buried in Las Vegas with a military headstone. Born abt. 1834 in England, his parents were from France. His surname spelling includes Gbill, Fruville, Truville, deFruville and so on.

Pct. 24 La Liendre, teacher Erculano Garcia[16]
Pct. 18 San Lorenzo, teacher Jesus Maria Gallegos y Martinez
Pct. 22 Sabinoso, teacher Jose Pablo Garcia

September 20, 1880- (teachers)
Pct. 10, Juan F. D. Frouville
Pct. 18, Gonzalo Ruiz[17]
Pct. 22, Jose Pablo Garcia
Pct. 24, Jose Leon Martines[18] (La Liendre)

March 4, 1882- (paid $40 plus $5 for house rent)
Pct. 10, Gregorio Flores paid $61
Pct. 22, Manuel Marquez

October 23, 1882-
Pct. 10, Isidoro Trujillo
Pct. 18, Louis Hommell[19]
Pct. 22, Jose Nestor Leyva

October 3, 1883-	Overseer	Teacher
Pct. 10	Ezequiel C de Baca	Manuel Armijo
Pct. 18	Luis Hommell	Leo Chavez
Pct. 22	Patrisio Gonzales	Presentasion D. Vigil[20]

In Precinct 24, District 18, Severo Tapia billed as the District Treasurer for $147.30 for doors, hauling adobes, taking the census and supervision of the schools. Tapia lived at La Liendre all his life and is buried at the Cañada de Aguilar.

Alice Blake taught school at Chaperito in 1900, she was a Presbyterian Missionary who later moved to Trementina where she helped build the school, infirmary and community center.

---

[16] Appears to have come from the Mora area to teach school.
[17] The 1870 census notes him as born in Mexico, age 39 and an adobe mason living in Rio Colorado.
[18] Likely the same man married to Maria Juliana Tapia at La Liendre in 1867.
[19] The 1880 census notes him as 48, a printer and from Saxony.
[20] Possibly the same person noted in the Ute Creek 1880 census, age 20 and a sheep raiser.

Chaperito Postmasters

Name	Title	Date Appointed
Frederick De Fruville	Postmaster	01/06/1875

discontinued on November 10, 1875
reestablished on December 27, 1875

Name	Title	Date Appointed
Gregoris Florez	Postmaster	12/27/1875
Francisco Robledo	Postmaster	12/18/1876
Jose Lucero	Postmaster	03/14/1877
Francisco Robledo	Postmaster	08/06/1877

discontinued on October 8, 1877
reestablished on January 30, 1880

Name	Title	Date Appointed
Adolph Straus	Postmaster	01/30/1880
Abe Goldsmith	Postmaster	12/05/1881
Samuel H. Bowman	Postmaster	12/08/1885
Francisco E. Robledo	Postmaster	06/19/1889
Frederick De Fruville	Postmaster	07/23/1890

discontinued on November 16, 1891
reestablished on May 6, 1892

Name	Title	Date Appointed
Carlos Martinez	Postmaster	05/06/1892
Jesus M. Martinez	Postmaster	07/16/1897
Betty Gunst	Postmaster	05/29/1901
Herculano Garcia	Postmaster	07/17/1908
Manuel Gonzalez	Postmaster	04/28/1909
Sostenes Delgado	Postmaster	04/11/1914
Eduardo Duran	Postmaster	02/28/1918
Francisco Arellanes	Acting Postmaster	01/31/1922
Francisco Arellanes	Postmaster	09/01/1922
Adolfo C. Garduño	Acting Postmaster	01/31/1955
Adolfo C. Garduño	Postmaster	02/10/1956

Discontinued on January 11, 1957; mail to Las Vegas
(Postal Bulletin 1-10-1957)

Military at Hatch's Ranch

Hatch's Ranch located on the west side of the Gallinas River was rented to the military from Alexander Hatch from 1856 to 1862. Companies E and K, 8th U. S. Infantry were here briefly around May 1860. The named changed to Chapman in 1879-80 as their first postman was John L. Chapman, the mail was discontinued here on April 15, 1879 and then picked up at Chaperito.[21] Rumors were that this area was a dispersal point for stolen livestock by Indians in Texas. Due to Hatch's Ranch and its connection with Fort Union, Chaperito was a good *puesto* (military post) for activities heading in all directions.

This small garrison was used to protect the settlers from Comanche and Kiowa raids. On the road between Fort Smith, Arkansas and Fort Sumner, Hatch's Ranch was also home to a „spy company" in 1861 based on rumors that the Confederates were advancing up the Pecos River. Travelers going from Santa Fe to Fort Sumner would use the road which was also used for distribution of supplies.[22]

Various Military Reports:

On July 7, 1847 a report was made that seventeen well-armed Kiowa mounted and armed all under the age of thirty were headed into Navajo country. The Commanding Officer, with all the men he could gather dispatched ten men and some thirty citizens from Las Vegas in protecting the people in that vicinity.

September 20, 1855, Hatch's Ranch was under attack by two hundred fifty strong (Comanche) who caused great injury and damage to the stocks and fields.

Reports dated 1858 mention many Comanche Indians in the vicinity of Chaperito. Spies were employed to monitor their whereabouts and on January 20, 1859, hundreds were seen near the Canadian River. On July 24, 1860, Companies E and K encountered about 450 – 500 Comanche near the Conchas, where they were camped and had intentions of heading east 50 miles from some location near Hatch's Ranch.

On October 3, 1860, Company K, 8th U. S. Infantry fought Comanche at Chaperito killing two. On May 29, 1861, Company E, a Regiment of Mounted Rifles fought with Comanche near the area reporting one Indian killed and three captured.[23]

In February 1865, Felix Ulibarri, a merchant at Chaperito, reported that a soldier from Company C, became drunk at a dance and abused several citizens in the village. The men allegedly entered homes, demanded whiskey and used profanity with Ulibarri's

---

[21] Julyan, Robert. *"The Place Names of New Mexico."* Pg. 77
[22] Rathbun, Daniel D. B. & David V. Alexander. *"New Mexico Frontier Military Place Names,"* 2003, Yucca Tree Press, Las Cruces, NM. Pgs. 38, 83-84,
[23] New Mexico State Records Center & Archives, Santa Fe, NM. Schroeder Papers, folders 1713, 1714, 1717.

wife Felipa. At that time, the soldiers discharged their rifles and pushed and beat their Lt. Charles Marion.[24]

In the Santa Fe Weekly Gazette, Saturday July 28, 1866, Capt. Rufus C. Vose, 1st Calvary, California Volunteers, reported that on June 14th, they left from Las Vegas, via Los Valles de San Agustin making note of the death of Miguel Gonzales.[25] Gonzales had gone out on the mesa three or four miles from the town to look after some stock, while on foot and with a Colt Pistol he was waylaid from behind by some Indians. Gonzales was clubbed and then shot with his own pistol. Near his hidden body were a Navajo blanket and the cross poles of a loom, a flat stick, all having blood on them. The Indians apparently took a number of horses and went in the direction of Cañon Largo.

A military roster taken at Chaperito, San Miguel County by Captain Manuel Flores, Co. C, 2nd Regiment, 2nd Brigade, 2nd Division, NM Milita notes the following soldiers who enlisted October 17, 1861 by Brig. Gen. Baca:

> Capt. Manuel Flores
> 1st Sgt. Gregorio Gallegos
> 2nd Sgt. Benito Baca
> Ensign rumaldo Lopes
> 1st Sgt. Cruz Apodaca
> 2nd Sgt. Marcelino Crespin
> 3rd Sgt. Polonio Duran
> 4th Sgt. Placido Apodaca
> 1st Cpl. Manuel Montoya
> 2nd Cpl. Candelario Gallegos
> 3rd Cpl. Nicolas Mestas
> 4th Cpl. Ascencio Saiz
> Drummer Suercio Lucero, 18
> Fifer, Ysidro Gallegos, 18
> 1. Pvt. Desederio Apodaca, 23
> 2. Pvt. Pedro Aragon, 25
> 3. Pvt. Francisco Baca, 33
> 4. Pvt. Juan de Jesus Chacon, 30
> 5. Pvt. Anastacio Duran, 24
> 6. Pvt. Marcos Garcia, 21
> 7. Pvt. Gabriel Gonzales, 42
> 8. Pvt. Matias Gonzales, 46
> 9. Pvt. Agapito Gonzales, 29
> 10. Pvt. Ricardo Garcia, 31
> 11. Pvt. Rafael Garcia, 31
> 12. Pvt. Nofrio Gallegos, 22

---

[24] Thompson, Jerry D. *"New Mexico Territory During the Civil War"*. University of New Mexico Press, 2008. Pgs. 75-75, 229.

[25] Author"s Note: Miguel Albino Gonzales was born between 1804-1814; he married to Maria Fabiana Blea they had nineteen known children. He is buried in the church at Los Valles de San Augustine.

13. Pvt. Ricardo Gallegos, 31
14. Pvt. Nepomucino Lucero, 42
15. Pvt. Juan Maria Lucero, 21
16. Pvt. Gabriel Lucero, 35
17. Pvt. Esquipula Lucero, 35
18. Pvt. Camilio Montaño, 28
19. Pvt. Jesus Muñis, 21
20. Pvt. Rafael Munis, 30
21. Pvt. Martin Montaño, 30
22. Pvt. Juan Madril, 18
23. Pvt. Desederio Martines, 25
24. Pvt. Manuel Montaño, 34
25. Pvt. Juan Antonio Montoya, 24
26. Pvt. Mariano Martines, 45
27. Pvt. Jesus Martines, 30
28. Pvt. Nicolas Martines, 42
29. Pvt. Pedro Ortega, 20
30. Pvt. Juan Antonio Ortega, 30
31. Pvt. Jesus Quesada, 30
32. Pvt. Pablo Rivera, 24
33. Pvt. Juan Andres Romero, 22
34. Pvt. Jose de la Cruz Sandoval, 25
35. Pvt. Julian sena, 35
36. Pvt. Antonio Aban Salasar, 30
37. Pvt. Teodocio Salas, 30
38. Pvt. Andres Salas, 23
39. Pvt. Refugio Torres, 21
40. Pvt. Pedro Varod, 32
41. Pvt. Jose Maria Varos, 35
42. Pvt. Rafael Valdes, 18
43. Pvt. Marcelino Varos, 28
44. Pvt. Francisco Candelario, 43

[7-742.]

Page No. **1**
Supervisor's District No. _____
Enumeration District No. **68**

Eleventh Census of the United States.

SPECIAL SCHEDULE.

SURVIVING SOLDIERS, SAILORS, AND MARINES, AND WIDOWS, ETC.

Persons who served in the Army, Navy, and Marine Corps of the United States during the war of the rebellion (who are survivors), and widows of such persons, in *San Agustin etc*, County of *San Miguel*, State of *New Mex*, enumerated in June, 1890. *Jose D. Martinez*, Enumerator.

House No.	Family No.	Names of Surviving Soldiers, Sailors, and Marines, and Widows.	Rank	Company	Name of Regiment or Vessel	Date of Enlistment	Date of Discharge	Length of Service (Yrs. Mos. Days)	
1	38	44	Miguel Martinez	Sergeant	L	= = Cav	= Sep 1864	= Sep 1866	2 0 0
2	53	59	Miguel Venavides	Sergeant	E	= = Cav	= Oct 1861	= Nov 1867	6 = =
3	59	65	Juan P Garcia	Private	=	= = Cav	= Sept 1861	= Mar 1862	0 6 0
4	101	109	Jose Anaya	Private	D	= = Inf	= Nov 1864	18 Sep 1867	3 0 19
5	104	112	Jose Peña	Private	=	= = Cav	= Nov 1860	= June 1861	0 9 0
6	144	153	Espiridion Sanchez	Sergeant	G	Kitbans Cav	1 Oct 1865	28 Nov 1868	3 1 28
7	196	206	Richard B. Martin	Private	E	15 Mich Inf	= Mar 1864	= Sep 1864	0 6 0
8	201	211	Francisco Lucero	Private	=	= = Cav	15 Sep 1861	15 Mar 1862	0 6 0
9	214	227	Jose R Ulivarri	Lt.	H	= = Cav	1 Feb 1862	30 Apr 1862	0 3 0
10	258	272	Antonio D. Revol	Private	A	= = Cav	= Sep 1861	= Feb 1862	0 6 0
11	299	315	Felez Garcia	Private	F	1 Reg Cav	= July 1861	= Aug 1864	3 1 0
12	300	316	Frederick De Fruville	Private	H	1 Col Cav	16 Sep 1863	7 Sep 1865	1 11 9

	Post-office Address	Disability Incurred	Remarks	
	10	11	12	
1	Las Vegas			1
2	Do			2
3	Las Vegas			3
4	Do			4
5	Chaperito	Sickness		5
6	Chaperito			6
7	East Las Vegas			7
8	Las Vegas			8
9	Chaperito			9
10	Las Vegas	Loss of Sight - By a shot shut		10
11	Chaperito			11
12	Chaperito	Chronic Rheumatism		12

11th Census of the US – 1890 Veterans Schedule, taken at San Agustin, NM; Ancestry.com

1860 Census of the Area

The census taker for this area did a roundabout circuit when he was taking the enumeration. Many of these small villages never appeared in the 1870 census and even less by 1880. It appears that some were incorporated into their larger neighbors. The 1860 census is in dwelling order as follows:

Jorupa (La Concepcion)
El Tecolotito
Hatch's Ranch+
Los Luceros*
El Aguila
Chaperito
Los Torres
Los Lajas*
La Liendre (San Antonio)
San Agustin
Cañada de Aguilar
Taylor Ranch*[26]
Mt. Pleasant*[27]
Lower Las Gallinas*

The 1860 Census notes many of these families occupied as freighters, laborers, wagon owners and foreigners; possibly all related to Hatch's Ranch and Ft. Union.

La Cueva+
Los Esteritos+
Ojos Chupaines*
Loma de Montosa*
Chupaines*[28]

Located somewhere between La Cueva and El Cerrito

El Cerrito
La Cuesta
El Salitre* (located south of Corazon and Cabra Springs)

*Not in 1870 Census
+ Not in 1880 Census

By 1880, the settlements of Sabinoso, San Lorenzo and Trementina begin to appear and in 1900, Los Fuertes appears although it had been inhabited for over 50 years.

---

[26] The 1860 Census has John M. Taylor, age 38, enumerated first, a farmer from Ohio, with real estate valued at $90,000. In 1880, he's a freighter living in Anton Chico.
[27] The 1860 Census notes a Levy Kiffly, age 50, farmer, born in Missouri as the first dwelling at Mount Pleasant. Unable to find him in further censuses.
[28] Possibly named after the Chipayne Apaches who wandered over eastern New Mexico and parts of west Texas. Mesa Apache is slightly northwest of Mesa Chupinas (current spelling).

Los Valles de San Augustine

Los Valles or San Augustin. This tiny inhabited village appears on most maps as San Agustin or more formally Los Valles de San Agustin; a prominence named San Agustin is 2 miles NE.[29] Los Valles (San Agustin), sacramental records attended by Anton Chico until 1876 then by Chaperito beginning in 1878 and first noted as a chapel up to 1880. On September 6, 1869, Jose Albino Madrid et al, deeded over to Juan Bautista Lamy lands at Los Valles for a church, the three plazas and cemetery for a sum of five pesos. It was also signed by Pedro Marques, Francisco Leger as commissioners and J. Pablo Madrid, Justice of the Peace.[30] The first baptism noted was for Zenon Padia, June 26, 1857, son of Rafael Padia and Ana Maria Lopez.

Los Valles, Church of San Augustine

---

[29] Julyan, Robert, "The Place Names of New Mexico", Pg. 309 San Miguel; settlement 9 miles SE of Las Vegas, on the Gallinas River; PO as Lourdes, 1918-66, mail to Las Vegas.
[30] San Miguel County Clerk's Office, Deed Books, September 6, 1869, a *capilla* deeded to the church, recorded November 7, 1894; Book 46 D, pg. 17.

This area was settled by 1841 when records indicate residents were prioritizing their water rights and by 1845 were enumerated in the Mexican census as Bayes de San Agustin with 127 individuals. Most of these early settlers migrated from San Miguel del Bado. An early fortress located a couple of miles northwest of Los Valles called Los Fuertes was home to Santiago Blea who was born at El Cerrito but migrated with his parents as a young man. Santiago later converted to Presbyterian and founded the site of Trementina.

Buried inside the church are Miguel Albino Gonzales, 1866; his son, Marcos Gonzales, a daughter-in-law and a priest. Oral history is that the church had a flat roof which was used as a defensive measure for Indian attacks.

Los Valles de San Augustin *Camposanto*:

Josefa Alasa 1870 88
Fernando J. Allemand
Bauno Analla 28 Oct 1880
Ignacia Angel 3 Apr 1908

Juanita Baca 18 Feb 1869
M. Lorenza Baca 22 Apr 1875
J. Macedon Balverde 1869 J. la 5
Barbarita Blea Nov 5 ___
C. A. Blea 21 Mch 1915
Candelaria Blea 21 Mch 1915
Gallestana Blea 15 Aug 1881
J. Blea Ab de 1882 PLS Eno
Jose Efre Blea 24 Feb 1923
Marselino Blea 20 Jly 1877
Rosario Blea 16 Nov 1892
Stacia Blea
Victor Blea 14 _lr AD 1898
Vleli Blea 21 Nov 1882

Manuel Ignacio Ca___ 21 Oct 1890
Filomino Coriz Co. F; In M. Inf

Juan Domices 3 Apr 1905
Bonifacia Duran 20 Jly 1895
Mafge Duran 30 Jan 1885
Maria Bersabela Duran 9 Jan 1882

T. G. 23 Nov 1898
Frank Gonzales Garcia NM Cpl 341 Inf WWI; 29 Feb 1824 – 22 Jan 1947

J. Hilario Garcia 14 Oct 1898
Jose Felis Ga___ 18 Apr 1882
Carmelita Garcia 26 Nov 1915
Encarnacion Garcia 6 Apr ___
J. S. Garcia Juan and___res
Jose Miguel Garcia 5 Apr 1887
Juan Pablo Garcia 2 May 1903
Ma Niebres Q. de Garcia 5 May 1914; 58 yr 6 mo
Marselio Garcia 10 Jne 1888
Mario Emilio Garsia 11 Sep 1885
Ricarda Garcia 12 Nov 1898
Roman Garcia 2 Oct 1930
Ruperta Garcia 20 Nov 1898
Victoria Garcia 22 Dec „98
Carolina Glesuberia 21 Nov 1898

Alonso Gonzales 6 4 of 1931
Andelesia Gonzales 6 Jne 1907
Benito Gos., 28 Nov _
Clayonces Robeyto Gonzales 16 Dec 1948
F. Ca. Garcia 19 Nov „98
J. B. Gonzales

J. Lion Gonzales 18 Feb 1879 E. ON. 31 May 1872 MNS
Jose Feles Gonzales 7 oct 1891
Jose Sabel Gonzales 21 June 1907
Jose Ynes Gonzales Aug 5 1898 – 5 Dec __
Juan G. Gonzales 3 Nov 1913
Juanita Gonzales 20 Jne 1891
Juana Maria Gonzales 18 Mch 1914
M. Anbrosia Gonzales Oct 18 „75
M. Isidora Gonzales 27 Mch 1887
Marcos Gonzales 15 Jan 1900
Martina S. Gonzlaes 1860 – 1 Feb 1933; 77/71 yr
Nbrocia Gonzales 8 Dec of 75
Otagracia Gonzales 1897 - 1976
P. Gonzales 31 May 1898
R. Gonzales 18 of 6 of 1907; _____ 2 days
Regino Gonzales 1 Sep 1867 – 17 Mch 1938 b. and d. in San Agustin
Rejino L. Gonzales 27 Nov 1922; 5 months 1 day
Remedia Gonzales 22 Apr 1968; 87 yr 7 mo 7 da
Idalia Gonza____ 2 June 1915
Trenidar Gonzales 23 Nov 1822; 4 years 20 days
Valentin Gonzales 5 Oct 1926
Ramon Goz 23 Nov „98
___acio Gurule 28 Feb 1911
Dominco Gurule 1806 – 27 Dec 1889
Lucia Gurule 20 Nov 1898

M. Lionarda 5 Oct 1879
Albador Lobato 26 May 1887
S. Lo_to 28 Oct „86
Sirlia Lobata 2 Aug 1882
Agustin J. Lucero 20 Sep 1890
Eloisa Lucero 13 Nov 1922
Juanita B. Lucero 1853 – 3 Apr 1934
Ceclia Doretea Lujan 10 Nov 1920
J. Lyon 6 Nov 1875

Demetrio Madrid 29 Dec 1890
M. Mta. Madrid 1 Sep 1887

Perciliano Madrid 18 Jly 1903
Jose Marquez
Romola G. Mart. 7 E 22 F Agsto 27
Romola C. D. Martinez 24 Oct 1922
Candelario Mestas 11 Nov 1894
M. Frnca Munis 1869 Feb 18

Tereza Q. N____28 Jly 1881

Bredeleno Quintana Nov 1898
Gregorio Quintana 26 Oct 1916
Juan Quintana 30 Aug 1907
Julianita G. de Quintana 28 Jne 1925
M. Quirina Quintana 19 Jne 1912; 51 yr
Ma. Nievez Quintana 5 May 1914; 58 yr
Marcos Quintana 23 Aug 1915
Teodora Quintana 2 Nov 1895
Tomacita Quintana 13 Jan 1896; 22 yr 10 mo 7 da

Isidro Romero 10 May 1890
Felix Romo Wyoming, Pvt. 166 Depot Brig. 17 Aug 1939
Solomon Romo 10 Oct 1922; 13 yr 18 mo 13 da
M. Ru____Sep 1877 (crumbling)
____Saiz

Alberia Saiz De R a de 189_ Linoma
Ambrocia Saiz 15 Oct 1908
Cornelio Saiz 9 Sep 1915; 68 yr 28 da
Dorot. Saiz 5 Aug 1909
Felonis Saiz 26 Jly 1920
I B. Saiz
Jose A. Sais 5 Dec 1901
Luciano Saiz 25 Nov 1918; 24 yr
Maria Pascualita Saiz 25 Apr 1905
P. Saiz   May 21 „30
Pertrita G. Saiz 27 Jly 1913; 25 yr 2 mo 4 da
Felis Salasar 21 Aug 1882
Juan Jose Salasar 18 Sep 1891

Josefa Talosa 88 fino
A Tapia Aug 22 1925; 3.6

Adela Tapia 12 Jly 1903
Guadalupita G. de Tapia 1 Sep 1903 – 14 Oct 1925
___L. Trujillo 23 May 1931
Agustin Trujio 14 Sep 1885
M. Trujillo 14 Apr 1888

Capina Vustos 20___sto 1882

Maria de los Angeles 19 Nov 1891 JLS
Jose_____25 Sep 1890

[taken byJean Whiting and Helen Hennon Sept. 1981, published by New Mexico Genealogy Society]

In 2009 less than a dozen of these are legible or there.

La Liendre
San Antonio

La Liendre, now a ghost town was settled prior to 1845 by people named Tapia, Martinez, Duran and Maes; it soon became the center of a Hispanic stock raising community, appearing in the 1850 census as Los Valles de San Antonio. Its present Spanish name means "nit, louse". One explanation for the name is that is described the community, where houses were strung along the roadside, "like nits". But residents were told that it referred to a local family with conspicuously small children "like nits".[31]

Chapel attended by church at Anton Chico from 1868, continuing as a chapel up to 1879 by Chaperito; records starting with 1880 the church is known as San Antonio. In May 1834, a baptism is noted at San Miguel del Bado for someone living at San Antonio, this might have been the first notice of someone moving eastward away from San Miguel.

The *capilla* at San Antonio was deeded over on August 8, 1869 from Jose Lopez to Lamy and recorded on November 7, 1894 for the sum of five pesos. Witnesses were Desiderio Martin, Matias Duran and Jose Pablo Madrid as Justice of the Peace. On June 16, 1888, Jose Leon Martinez and Cirilio Delgado, commissioners for the Pueblo of La Liendre deed over the land for the cemetery for a sum of one peso. The said *camposanto* is found in the middle of land sort of made public, a little outside the center of the plaza to the northeast of the church. Dimensions are 50 yards' square with a door to the north. Signed Jose Leon Martinez, Cirilio Delgado, Hurbano Martinez and Jesus Maria Sanchez; Placido Apodaca signed as Justice of the Peace.[32]

The first postman at La Liendre was Manuel Baca in February 1878, Ezequiel C de Baca in September 1882 and then Felipe Tapia in May 1906.

---

[31] Julyan, Robert, "The Place Names of New Mexico", Pg. 190-91. San Miguel settlement; SE of Las Vegas, at the end of NM 67; PO 1878-80, 1882-84, 1906-42), mail to Las Vegas.
[32] San Miguel County Clerk's Office, Deed Book; deeded over on August 8, 1869, recorded November 7, 1894, Book 46, pg. 12. Graveyard recorded deed for Plaza de la Liendre, June 16, 1888, Book 35, pg. 508.

**Church in La Liendre, NM, photo by: Fritz Broeske,
Courtesy Palace of the Governors (MNM/DCA) Negative no. 120100**

Camposanto at La Liendre:

Juan Apodaca March 30 _____
Martina Benabides January 2 1899 – October 26 1898
Juanita D. Blea October 23 1901 -____9, 1922
Maria Tomasita Cedios December 3 1920; 6 years
Agapita de M. Delgado b. 1885 d. ____
M. E. Gallegos December 13 1899 – February 9 1920
Luisita Garcia August 23 1908; 11 years
Ana Maria Gomez July 5 1895 – September 30 1933
Emilia Herrera November 19 1898
Florencia Maez August 13 1911 – April 21 „29
Brigida Marquez 1896; 47 years
Estefana A. de Marquez Dec 24____- May 27 1949
Tereza F. Marquez   October 13 1916 – October 18____5
Antonia Martinez January 13 1913; 17 years
Antonio Martinez
Caslos Martines March 26 1883
Deciderio Martinez September 28 1904; 73 years 7 months 17 days old
Donaciana Martinez October 24 1939; Pvt 49 Inf.
J. Lorenzo Martinez August 10 1922 – February 27 1924
Juan T. Martinez January 17 1886

Juanito Martinez b. April 4 1920 d. May 26 1920
Justa Rufina Montolla 1833 – 1918
Augstin Quintana March 12 1895 – May 4 1901; 75 years
Apolonia Ramirez 1910
Anjelina Tapia June 27 1904
Cayetano Tapia b. August 7 1866 d. Jan ____
Desiderio Tapia Co. F INM Cav
Domitilia Tapia b. July 5 1908
Francisquita B. de Tapia April 2 1906
Juan G. Tapia 1952
M. J. Tapia September 23 1922
Tomasita Tapia b. December 29 1876 d. April 15 1905

      Large family groups migrated to this area from San Miguel del Bado. Jose Domingo Martinez (Maria Antonia Gonzales) and the family of Salvador Tapia intermarried quite a bit; many times brothers of one family marrying sisters of another. The bulk of these cemetery findings are all tied to these families. Domingo Martinez (1824-1900) married a second time to Rebecca Marquez, widening his family in the area with sixteen known children. Salvador Tapia (1790-1866) married three times and had fifteen known children. His first wife, Maria Luz Estrada, 2nd, Maria Nieves Sisneros and 3rd Ana Maria Gomez.

Los Torres

Los Torres, this former settlement now abandoned and part of a large ranch, recalls a family name in the area.[33] The first baptism noted in Anton Chico for Los Torres was that of Maria Sista Torres, August 1860, daughter of Refugio Torres and Maria de los Remedios Duran. This family remained here for some time and may well be the namesake of the area. The graveyard was deeded to the church on October 31 1877.

San Jose is their patron saint and the church was attended by Chaperito beginning in 1880; prior church records are in Anton Chico church. The first recorded baptism at Anton Chico regarding Los Torres was that of Maria Leonara Angel on December 14, 1858, daughter of Eugolio Angel and Maria Dolores Ribera.

In 1860, Los Torres had twenty-four dwellings and sixty-six people. Enumerated right after Chaperito, we find that some of the original land grantees were actually living at Los Torres.

The area known as **Las Lajas** was named in the land grant as one of the settlements and is in the 1860 census after Los Torres with fourteen households. The enumeration does show that land grantees were living here and not at Chaperito. Currently location of this area has not been found to date, but by 1870 it was incorporated into Los Torres. The first recorded baptism in Anton Chico for Las Lajas was Maria Petra Rael, May 1, 1858, daughter of Juan Rael and Manuela Duran.

Los Fuertes, a community north of Los Valles on the Gallinas River[34] is a huge fortress that was used by many families in the mid-1800"s to combat the Indians and provide shelter for those that decided to live there. Their migration was from San Miguel del Bado and Los Cerritos. The first noted baptism was for Teodora Valverde on November 29, 1959, daughter of Macedon Valverde and Maria Dolores Mestas. Many later moved to Trementina after they converted religion. Coming back around 1910, they disassembled the church, took the flagstone and re-built La Paz Church at Trementina.[35]

---

[33] Julyan, Robert, "*The Place Names of New Mexico*", Pg. 211. San Miguel County settlement 19 miles SE of Las Vegas, on the N bank of the Gallinas River.
[34] Julyan, Robert, "The Place Names of New Mexico", Pg. 209. Located 9 miles SE of Romeroville on the E bank of the Gallinas River. Abandoned Hispanic Community whose Spanish name means "the forts."
[35] Gonzales, Samuel Leo. *"The Days of Old."* pg. 13.

Ruins at Los Fuertes – Plaza type fortress

Walls at Los Fuertes

La Concepcion
Los Jacales, possibly named Jorupa

La Concepcion has some remains of an isolated Hispanic community, whose name honors the Immaculate Conception.[36] In the Catholic Directory, Los Jacales drops off and La Concepción remains and uses the same patron saint; attended by Anton Chico in 1866 then Chaperito from 1880. The church has been under restoration for many years now on the road between Los Valles and La Liendre. The official Catholic Directory notes Concepcion's church as Immaculate Conception starting in 1915. A baptism for Jorupa noted in Anton Chico was done for Jose Crespin Apodaca, October 29, 1859, son of Manuel Esquipula Apodaca and Serafina Jaramillo. On December 15, 1876, Carlos Martinez and Carlota Leger deeded forever a chapel to J. B. Lamy for a sum of one peso.[37] Graveyard deeded to Jacales on May 26, 1877, but possibly never recorded.

Church at La Concepcion

Concepcion *Camposanto*:   July 29, 1998

AA Allemand   October 18 1898 – December 10 1898
Rio de Paloin Arguello 1898; 50 days
Bpahm d. 1845
Carmelita Baros   July 29 1920
Ocilia Baros 1909
Samuel Baros
Ocilia Baros d. 1909

---

[36] Julyan, Robert, "*The Place Names of New Mexico*", Pg. 188. San Miguel County settlement; 13 miles SE of Romeroville, on the N bank of the Gallinas River; PO 1882-85, mail to Las Vegas.
[37] San Miguel County Clerk"s Office, Deed Book, recorded December 26, 1894, Book 44, pg. 180.

Eugia Garcia   November 27 1898; 15 years 8 months 26 days
Frca Fidelia Garcia age 2 years 18 days
Ines Gonzales   April 20 1848 - July 10 1915
Jacob Jaramillo 1939
Florentina Leger   April 25 1918
Benigna Lujan   July 13 1923; 63 years
Lucio Lujan   December 27 1898; 5 years old
Elvira Martinez died 1889, born 1880
Momokaie Martinez died the 9th
Petrita Muniz 1915; 70 years
Eulalia Ortega died December 1891
Marto Padia November 22 ____
Bernardita Quintana May 11 1830 – September 26 1993
Eduardo Quintana March 30 1830 – September 26 1993
Jesus Quintana October 1860 – October 1926
Juan Quintana   November 19 1925; 74 years
Marita Dulcienea Quintana January 27 1921; 12 years
Victoria Romero November 11 1928
Juan Cristobal Romo December 29 1888
Felipita Senta____13 1992, born May 1 1881
Aniceto Tapia December 8 1824; 60 years

La Aguila

Aguila is an abandoned settlement, whose Spanish name means "eagle.[38] First noted at El Aguila in the 1860 Census with nineteen dwellings and 76 inhabitants. In 1870, Los Luceros disappears from the census, but could be one of the settlements on the other side of the river. The area had grown to thirty-four dwellings by this time. Based on the number of ruins and foundations, this was a rather large community at one time.

First attended by Chaperito in 1916 with a Catholic Church, records mostly at Anton Chico and as St. Anthony Church. The settlement is built in a defensive pattern with four sides and long high walls half way up a mesita. The remains are on both sides of the Gallinas River with the major part of the site on the west and the church and *camposanto* on the east. All that remains is one headstone that of Necolas Maestas within a large walled *camposanto*. Dry rock fencing for the sheep runs along the embankments of the Gallinas River.

The Presbyterian movement had brought Miss Young a teacher and missionary where she lived at El Aguila, she was getting ready to retire and Alice Blake was chosen to replace her. Miss Blake oversaw the mission and an evangelist, Teofilo Tafoya, encouraged her. She starting dividing her time between La Aguila and Trementina, but it became difficult for her to travel that 30 miles' distance. Miss Blake was known to call people who secured title to the public lands as "land-grabbers," and realized that people were moving east for better conditions. She eventually made her way to Trementina and many of the converted Presbyterians moved with her; names include: Pablo Madrid, Norberto Jaramillo, Abran Salazar, Romulo Blea, Santiago Blea and Cecilio Valverde.

---

[38] Julyan, Robert, "*The Place Names of New Mexico*", Pg. 6. San Miguel County; settlement on the E bank of the Gallinas River, 2 miles SE of Chaperito.

Cañada de Aguilar

The migration pattern from San Miguel del Bado eastward falls generally in this area known as Aguilar. Located within the boundaries of the Antonio Ortiz Land Grant, southwest of La Liendre, Aguilar is but ruins and an old *camposanto*. A creek and a small spring are located near the area. Surrounded by mesas on three sides, the twelve dwellings documented in the 1860 census account for forty-eight people, the site remained small up to 1870 with ninety-one households and growing into the early 1900''s. Inhabitants used the church at San Miguel del Bado, Anton Chico, Chaperito and La Liendre. The Chaperito Land Grant names the mesita de Aguilar as a boundary marker. The first noted baptism in Anton Chico is that of Margarita Muñiz, February 26, 1860, daughter of Jesus Muñiz and Maria del Refugio Tapia.

Aguilar *Camposanto*:

Aniseta Aragon August 31 1914; 53 years 4 months 21 days
Antonio Blea October 4 1921 & Marcelino Blea July 9 1913, 1 year 1 month 7 days, (one headstone over the other)
Pedro Blea January 14 1925; 23 years 8 months 5 days old
J. C. G.
P. S. G. September 6 1921
Florencia Garcia March 2 – April 30 1920
Florentina Garcia March 12 1913; 1 year 11 months 28 days old
Jose Maria Garcia February 10 1916; 11 months 17 days old
Remijio M. Garcia September 4 1887 - December 21 1915; 48 years 3 months 17 days
Rita Garcia September 4 1880 – June 20 1918; 37 years 9 months 16 days old
Severiana Garcia September 18 1917 - December 17 1922
Albinita M. de Gomez July 20 1912; 22 years 4 months 20 days old
Dolores de Gomez November____1906; 72 years
Epimenia Gomez June 29 1906; 4 years
Florencio Gomez July 6 1906; 4 years
Juan Gomez November 11 1904; 19 years
Juanita Gomez   June 29 1906
Marillita Gmez January 22 1916
Margarito Gomez
Pasesita Gomez January 25 1924 - August 3 1924
Maria Salomon Gomez
Teoduro Gomez
Federico Herrera November 12 November 1948
Ignacita G. Martinez April 4 1920; 35 years 2 months 2 days old
Guadalupe Quintana December 25 1913; 23 years 11 months 13 days old
Juanita L. Tapia June 19 1902 – December 11 1927
Severo Tapia November 1 1858 – January 16 1922

Felicitas A. Urioste February 10 1914; 56 years
Fidel Urioste October 29 1908 – April 3 1923
Isabel Urioste January 28 1914
Simon Urioste
No Name July 10 1913, 1 year 1 month old
Gregorio Fidiroa January 8 108; 22 years

Taken September 1983 by Jean Whiting and confirmed April 2009 by author. Some headstones have weathered and are illegible today.

Ranches & Farms of the Lower Gallinas
Las Gallinas Spring

Gallinas Spring a former community, named for its association with *Ojo de Las Gallinas*.[39]

The small *camposanto* is located on the western side of the Gallinas River with many abandoned houses and a three to four-foot flagstone fence that runs along the river likely for herding sheep. The buried settlers are located in the 1860 census known as Lower Gallinas, 1870 as Gallinas Crossing Ranch and into 1880 only as a Precinct. This group appears to have migrated from San Miguel del Bado having been married there prior to moving east. The *camposanto* is large but only a few headstones remain. Records associated with these individuals also appear in La Aguila. Church records recognize this area as Las Gallinas Spring, a station attended by Chaperito starting in 1915.

Lower Gallinas *Camposanto*:

Terecita Alarid January 25 1916
Anita Tafoya January 1904
Josefa Alarid May 9 1897
Aurelio Samora February 6 1898
Encarnacion Alarid 1891

---

[39] Julyan, Robert, "The Place Names of New Mexico", Pg. 143. San Miguel County settlement; in S part of county, 7 miles S of Chaperito; PO 1874-1906, mail to Chaperito.

San Lorenzo
Lopezville

San Lorenzo, a military outpost during the American occupation, this settlement, now abandoned, was named by Lorenzo Lopez to commemorate his patron saint and also his own name. Lopez was San Miguel County Sheriff in the late 1880"s.[40] San Lorenzo drops from the church rolls in 1924; first attended by Anton Chico in 1873, then in 1878 as a chapel by Chaperito.

Noted in the 1880 census, the village is much smaller by 1910 with eight dwellings and thirty-four inhabitants. San Lorenzo's church may have later been used by those at Chavez. It appears from the church records that Chavez also had the same patron saint St. Lawrence when it was documented in the Catholic Directory.

Chavez short-lived community took the name of its first postmaster, Francisco S. Chaves.[41] First appearing in the 1910 census as a very small community it continues being enumerated up to 1930.

---

[40] Julyan, Robert, "The Place Names of New Mexico", Pg. 317. San Miguel; settlement in E part of county, near Conchas Lake; PO 1876-77.
[41] Julyan, Robert, "The Place Names of New Mexico", Pg. 78. San Miguel settlement in E part of County, on the SW border of the Pablo Montoya Grant; PO 1901-1906, mail to Trementina.

El Cerro de Corazon

Corazon, now a ghost town, took its name from nearby El Cerro de Corazon. Corazon hill resembles a heart, especially when viewed from the west El Cerro del Corazon is not be confused with Corazon Hill just to the west, a long, steep highway descent from the mesas around Trujillo the valley below.[42] The church Sacred Heart was attended by Chaperito from 1890-1893, then noted in 1915 as Corazon

A February 11, 2002, Albuquerque Journal article notes many houses built along Corazon Creek. The *camposanto* has a metal archway with the name Corazon *Camposanto* overhead.[43]

A shrine to the Virgin Mary sits below the *cuesta* and before Corazon.

One document dated August 18, 1889 made by Hilario Romero to J. B. Salpointe deeds over some land for a *camposanto* for the sum on one dollar. The deed mentions it is for the sole use of a Catholic Church situated in the NE4, SE4, Sect 16, Township 14, NR 22 E and measures from north to south 35 feet and from east to west 61 feet with the following boundaries: on the north by a graveyard and the south, east and west the property of Hilario Romero.[44] A second document made by Antonio Gonzales and his wife, Manuelita V. de Gonzales, deeded to the church land for a chapel at El Corazon.[45]

Shrine to the Virgin Mary at the bottom of the *cuesta* near Corazon.

---

[42] Julyan, Robert, "The Place Names of New Mexico", Pg. 96. San Miguel); settlement 12 miles SE of Trujillo; PO 1903-1909, mail to Chaperito.
[43] Thompson, Fritz, Albuquerque Journal, "A Lost Heart", February 11, 2002, p. A1-A2
[44] San Miguel County Clerk's Office, Deed book 37, pg. 16. Coordinates are for Corazon.
[45] San Miguel County Clerk's Office, Deed Book. Recorded June 30, 1909, Book 67, pg. 114. Homesteaded land cert #2146. Same coordinates as Hilario Romero.

El Sabinoso

Sabinoso today is a small extremely isolated inhabited community the name likely taken from the local tree, the one-seed juniper.[46] The church Santo Niño and San Jose attended by Chaperito from 1890 then known as San Antonio and Santo Niño. In 1906 noted as Nuestra Señora de Guadalupe, which may be an error in updating the Catholic Directory. The church first stood on the east side of the Canadian River but after a major flood in the early 1900"s they moved it across to the west side. Two cemeteries mark the area, one near the old church site and one at Cañon Largo.

The town itself first appeared in the 1880 Census as Sabinosa and Sabinosaa. Settlers migrated from Rociada/ Mora and San Miguel del Bado via Chaperito.

Church at Sabinoso

Near the location of the first church are a handful of headstones, they are those of Ramon Lujan (1842-1911) and his wife Hilaria Gonzales (1846-1917). There are a few others that are partially illegible.

---

[46] Julyan, Robert, "The Place Names of New Mexico", Pg. 306, 181. San Miguel settlement; 5 miles N of US 419, on the Canadian River; PO 1913-28, 1939-74.

La Cinta
Santo Niño

La Cinta. This abandoned locality likely was named for La Cinta Creek, which heads 16 miles N of Bell Mountain and flows S past the Bell Ranch to join the Canadian River E of Conchas Reservoir.[47] The church, Santo Niño, attended by Chaperito from 1890.

La Cinta first appears in the 1880 census covering other areas such as Rio Colorado and Cabra Springs. In the 1900 census, Cabra Springs had their own section enumerated and La Cinta is not enumerated but may have been incorporated with another village.

---

[47] Julyan, Robert, "The Place Names of New Mexico", Pg. 85. San Miguel County settlement; in SE part of county, on the Pablo Montoya Grant; PO 1887-88, mail to Bell Ranch. Spanish, "ribbon, band, strip".

La Garita
Lower Canadian River Settlements

La Garita[48] was first attended from Chaperito in 1905 as a church noted as San Hilario, but later known as La Garrito and a station attended by Chaperito in 1915. Unknown location, but a small church is located one mile south of Variadero and known as La Garita area. The first Postman was appointed on January 19, 1907 and was Sixto Martinez. This small post office was first established as Variadero.

La Garita / San Ysidro

---

[48] Julyan, Robert, "The Place Names of New Mexico", Pg. 89, 371. San Miguel settlement current PO is Variadero; the Spanish *garita* has been translated variously as "lookout", "watchtower", "jail", and "sentry box or entrance to a town"

La Trementina
San Rafael Church

Not to be confused with the Presbyterian hamlet. San Rafael is about 3 miles NW of Old Trementina.[49] First attended by Chaperito from 1894-1912 as a station and in 1913 as a chapel.

The church and *camposanto* lands were donated by Rafael Sanchez and his wife, Maria Apolonia Ramirez. They moved to this area from Rincon de Tecolote (Rociada), homesteaded around 1895 and their descendants have remained ever since. Several families moved with them, Madrid, Maes and Romero. Apolonia is buried beneath the church floor.

San Rafael Church, interior

---

[49] Julyan, Robert, "The Place Names of New Mexico", Pg. 320, 358-59. San Miguel County settlement; at junction of NM 104 and 419, 15 miles E of Trujillo; PO 1901 to present.

San Rafael, *función* **Oct 2005**

Gate to *camposanto* and church of San Rafael and the donor of the land headstone.

The Year of 1908 — Contribution for the Church

Money for the wood	$1
Rafael Sanchez, money	$25
Hilario Gonzales, a hefer of one year	$27
one of two years	$12
Melecio Sanchez, a cow of two years	$15
Money	$5.50
Isabel Encinias, a cow of two years	$15
Money	$5
Sesario Sanchez, *un ternera de un año*	$12
Braulio Ramirez, money	$3
Trevino Ramirez, money	$5
Filberto Sanchez, money	$4
Balentin money	$5
Melecio Martinez, *un ternera de año*	$12
Money	$5.50
Manuel Garcia, 3 days of work	
Ricardo Gomez, money	$1
Vitor Gonzales, one she goat and money	$1.25
	$ .50
Sesario Gonzales, one goat and money	$1.25
	$ .50
Nicanor Archuleta, money	$3
Carlos E. Trujillo, *novilla de año*	$12
Carlos Trujillo, the bell for the church[50]	

Camposanto at La Trementina (San Rafael):

Apolonia Ramirez January 9 1860 – March 2 1920 inside church floor
Simona Chabes 1861 - 1940
Isabel Encinias 1873 - 1934
Rosenda T. Encinias March 1 1887 – September 15 1968
Victoriano Encinias September 30 1919 – July 13 1966
Manuelita Espinosa July 25 1864 – March 1942
Zolio Fresquez may 1928 – October 1 1940
Benerito Garcia 1942 - 1952
Bernarda Gonzales October 17 1888 – March 2 1922
Bitalia Lujan b. January 16 1930
Alcario Madrid January 20 1888 – February 26 1971
Carlota Madrid 1892 - 1943
Perfecto Madrid
Petra Madrid 1930
Rosinsa S. Madrid April 8 1866 – March 15 1915

---

[50] Author"s family records.

Valentin Madrid December 17 1875 – August 8 1837
Angela Maes July 1952 – October 1952
Daniel Maes August 1 1886 – September 28 1959
Delfino Maes December 25 1912 – April 5 1980
Maria Maes
Nicanor Domingo Maes August 3 1941 – November 26 1981
Paublita Maes January 15 1910 – October 4 1988
Filomen Martinez
Robert Gale Martinez 1963
Damion S. Mason March 21 1983 – March 30 1883
Apolonia Maria Pacheco 1933-1937
Emilia Pacheco November 29 1898 – October 3 1987
Emilio Pacheco April 6 1903 – January 5 1995
James Pacheco October 3 1962 – October 1 1940
Adela S. Padilla June 21 1905 – Sept. 12 1997
Jose L. Padilla 1876 - 1965
Nocario F. Padilla May 26 1903 – April 2 1975
Simon Padilla August 9 1911 – June 21 1983
Isabel Romero 1896 – 1996 (male)
Ninfa M. Romero 1908-1991
Alfonso Sanchez, Sr. 1907 – 2000
Cordelia J. Sanchez 1912 - 2000
Carlos L. Sanchez 1846 - 1989
Elisa Sanchez October 29 1888 – July 2 1959
Guadalupe Sanchez 1899 - 1967
Melecio Sanchez August 18 1874 – March 1 1964
Rafael Sanchez 1900-1953
Rafel Sanchez 1845-1916
Virginia L. Sanchez September 30 1878 – December 13 1977
Carlos Trujillo
Cristobal Trujillo 1907 – 1972
Larri C. Trujillo 1939 - 1976

Variadero
La Barriadero

Variadero was founded by Jose Lauriano Estrada about 1872. The name is local coinage from the Spanish to *variar*, to vary or change, referring here to frequent changes in the course of the Conchas River.[51] Sagrada Familia church first attended by Chaperito from 1894-1903; then in 1904 as a chapel.

Gate to *camposanto*, Variadero

Variadero has a historic bridge that was built around 1930, with concrete trusses.[52]

---

[51] Julyan, Robert, "The Place Names of New Mexico", Pg. 371. San Miguel County settlement; on Conchas River and NM 104; PO is Variadero 1907 intermittently to 1923, mail to Trementina; PO as Garita 1900-present.

[52] Rae, Steven R., Joseph E. King, Donald Abbe. *Historic Bridge Survey for the New Mexico Highway Department.* May 1984. NMSHD #3964, located on NM104, 50" span, length 200".

**Church interior, Variadero, NM, 1975, photo by Robert Brewer,
Courtesy Palace of the Governors (MNM/DCA) Negative no. 65146**

Variadero *Camposanto*:　　　　　　　　　　　　　　　　　　November 26, 1997

Cleofas S. Chavez 1900 – 1956
Feliz Chavez 1885 -1965
Donaciana (illegible) 1890 – 1981
Agapita Estrada d. 1955
Com Estrada November 27 1913
E. V. Estrada 72859-1944
Elias Estrada May 1895 – October 1892
Filomena M. Estrada, March 7 1929; 90 years
Jose Laureno Estrada March 19 1898; 65 years
Manuel Estrada 1917 - 1948
Marcela E. Estrada June 1917 – April 1957
Maria Isabel Estrada 1886 - 1948
Onofre Estrada September 9 1919 – October 27 1977
Jose Manuel Garcia
Margarito Garcia 1881 - 1856
Avelino Gonzales
Casimiro Gonzales 1856-1985

Fabiana L. Gonzales 1875 - 1904
Luciano Gonzales September 22
Raquei_ N. Gonzales October 1913 – May 8 1920
Teodorita Griego
Carmen O. Hicks 1942-1963
Cruz Lucero 1908 - 1979
Delfino Lucero November 1884 – February 1961
Fedelina Lujan 1928-1989
Francisquita Madrid 1867-1994
Maria Eufemia Maestas d. 1898
Maria Bernardo Martinez 11 months
Francisco Ortiz 1869-1945
Vienta Ortiz December 1889 -
Cliofes Quintana 1911 – 1977
Fernando Quintana 1876 - 1942
Juan N. Quintana 1869-1945
Julia S. Quintana 1929-1997
George Roybal March 1933 - January 1972
Pedro Roybal 1870 - 1943
Juan Sisneros June 1874 – June 1860
Chris Trujillo 1942 - 1995

Headstone of
Jose Lauriano Estrada, *"El Primer Poblador del Barriadero"* The first settler of Variadero. 1836-1898.

El Cañon Largo
Upper Canadian River Settlements

Cañon Largo's church was named San Acasio first attended from Chaperito in 1890. A large *camposanto* exists at this site.

A military camp was located here in the early 1860''s as this was rugged and remote area. Not inhabited for long, it continued to be a good overnight stop between Forts Union and Bascom.[53]

Records indicate lands were deeded to the church on May 19, 1880.[54]

---

[53] Rathbun, Daniel C. B. & David V. Alexander, "New Mexico Frontier Military Place Names." Pg. 29-30.
[54] San Miguel County Deed Book. Recorded September 8, 1885, Book 28, pg. 151.

San Ramon[55]

A small scatter of buildings, long abandoned; an abandoned church sits in ruins and *camposanto* near the main highway.

Cemetery at San Ramon

San Ramon *Camposanto*:

Mary Archuleta   October 5 1928 – April 28 1990
Lorenzo Archuleta   January 28 1928 – May 7 2008
Ines Blea   November 25 1918
Ramon E. Chavez, Cpl US Army, October 27 1910 – July 25 1994
Adela G. Encinias   1915-1949
Candelario Garcia   January 10 1916
Marillita Romero Garcia   November 24 1918
Pablo Garcia   October 1917
Paula Garcia   1911-1918
Eugenio Gonzales   November 15 1884 – July 6 1954
Florentino Gosales   b. 1900 d. July 10 1930 "Los Resjos"
Lieselotte S. Gonzales b. February 21 1930 Germany d. _ El Paso, TX "Pippie Girl Boom Booms"

Maria Reyes G. Gonzales   March 31 1891 – February 3 1968

---

[55] Julyan, Robert, "*The Place Names of New Mexico*," Pg. 320. San Miguel County settlement; on NM 419, 5 miles N of Trementina.

P. M.	May 13 „16
Nieves Madri	1854-1941
Agapito G. Quintana	April 11 1907 – July 22 1944
Eulalia M. Quintana	1899-1968
Ferminia J. Quintana	January 23 1853 – November 29 1926
Frances Quintana	May 6 1927 – Janurary 29 1969
Francisquita A. Quintana	1888 – 1961
Jose Quintana	January 23 1853 – November 29 1926
Pablita M. Quintana	1878-1951
Juan F. Quintana	June 24 1942 – July 21 1958
Petronilo Quintana	1875 – 1964
Ramon Quintana Pvt US Army WWI,	April 20 1897 – June 10 1992
Transito Quintana	October 31 1897 – October 4 1978
Ventura Quintana	1878-1959
Amelia E. Romero	May 4 "75"
Henry Romero	1886-1972
Basilia Q. Sanchez	1884-1963
Alfredo Sandoval	March 1904

Old church ruins at San Ramon

Sanchez[56]

Named after its first postmaster, Manuel A. Sanchez. Three headstones in the area: Lola Nolan 1878 – 1910; Antonio Sanchez 1836 – 1914 (6 ft. gray marble); 1877 (illegible marker). Founded as a ranching and farming center in the late 1800"s. Antonio Sanchez migrated from the Rociada area and homesteaded in this upper Canadian River area.

Ruins near Alamitos, an area where Comancheros would rest and barter.

---

[56] Julyan, Robert, "*The Place Names of New Mexico*," Pg. 320. San Miguel County settlement; on NM 419, 5 miles N of Trementina.

Arollo de las Conchas

Las Conchas[57] station attended by Chaperito from 1915. **Las Conchas Abajo** (Refuge of Sinners), attended by Chaperito from 1915. The church was burned and remnants survive. The *Camposanto* is still active. Noted as two different areas, but likely the same one.

This tiny isolated *camposanto* is near the Conchas River and Conchas Dam. The church and *camposanto* lie in a small valley with the Conchas River in the background. Longtime resident of San Rafael (Trementina), Alfonso Sanchez, Sr., mentioned that this Catholic *Camposanto* was used here because it was too far to Variadero.

Las Conchas *Camposanto*:

Name	Birth	Death
Anna Louise Baca	b. July 27, 1968	d. July 30, 1968
Maria Ternida Ortiz	b. Jan 30 1914	d. March 1919
Porfirio Tenorio		d. May 1, 1935
Dematia Tenorio	b. October 22, 1866	
Agustina Tenorio	b. April 14, 1895	d. February 8, 1944
Beatriz Tenorio	1899-1948	
Lucia elena Torres	b. January 9, 1918	d. November 11, 1936
Tomasita Tenorio	b. September 6, 1906	d. March 9, 1994
Jose Reducindo Roybal	b. July 26, 1907	d. October 29, 1990
Eugenio Roybal	b. November 13, 1899	d. September 17, 1999
Lorenzo Roybal	b. April 26, 1931	
Guadalupe Ortiz	b. November 21, 1925	d. May
Paulita Ortiz	b. June 18, 1887	d. September 25, 1984
Jose E. Ortiz	1879-1954	
Jose Ynez Ortiz	b. December 13, 1912	d. November 7, 1966
Mala Inez Lujan	b. November 29, 1966	d. November 21, 1985
Celina O. Lujan		d. February 28, 1933

---

[57] Juylan, Robert. "The Place Names of New Mexico," Pg. 92. San Miguel County, located near Conchas Lake and Conchas Dam. The Dam was built in 1937 by the US Army Corps of Engineers. This hamlet is located to the west of the lake.

San Hilario

Although this name commemorates St. Hilary, a 4th century Dr. of the Catholic Church, this former locality often was called simply Hilario and could in fact recall one Hilario Gonzales.[58] San Hilario attended by Chaperito from 1890-1904. It comes off the rolls under Chaperito. In its place is La Garita, which takes the name of the same patron saint. Possibly could be the same location or the chapel was washed away and residence started using La Garita or it could be a second San Hilario.

---

[58] Julyan, Robert, "The Place Names of New Mexico", Pg. 313. San Miguel settlement; near Conchas Dam; PO 1878-86, mail to La Cinta.

Other Missions served by Chaperito

Cherisco (El Choro), DeVriesas, Sabino -- all noted as stations in 1904-1915 and attended by Chaperito. Locations of these stations is unknown

Conchas Lake / Conchas Dam was built by the US Army Corps of Engineers in 1937 to impound the Canadian River. The confluence of the Conchas and Canadian Rivers now is submerged by the reservoir.[59]

El Cerro (Sacred Heart) -- first attended by Chaperito in 1894 as a chapel. Location unknown, although likely near Garita or Corazon.

El Mesteño (San Miguel) -- first attended by Chaperito in 1890. Located between Trementina and Sabinoso on the eastern plains.

Los Alamitos (San Ramon) -- attended by Chaperito in 1890. An old comanchero camp on the eastern side of San Ramon.

Los Alamosas (Holy Cross) -- first attended by Chaperito in 1890. Location unknown.

Mangas (St. Louis) -- attended by Chaperito in 1915. Location unknown.

Norias (San Ramon) -- first attended by Chaperito in 1904 as San Ramon chapel. Location unknown.

Tucumcari -- notation that they were building a church in 1904. This church typically falls under Santa Rosa starting in 1910.

---

[59] Julyan, Robert, *"The Place Names of New Mexico"*, Pg. 92-93

Other Place Names in Area

Salitre -- a non-inhabited area except for the 1860 census; means salt or salt peter. South of Cabra Springs near Corazon.

Trementina (La Paz Presbyterian Church) is usually depicted as the Presbyterian Community and ghost town located by Conchas Dam. The area was first settled by Santiago Blea and nine other founders who had recently decided to convert from Catholicism. Moving from Los Valles de San Augustin and Los Fuertes, they had herded their sheep in this area for many years prior to homesteading in the late 1870"s. Santiago Blea and his son-in-law Norberto Jaramillo were buffalo hunters, Santa Fe Trail travelers and sheep ranchers. The community was blessed to have a missionary Ms. Blake who devoted about 30 years of her life to live here and further the education, health and religious needs of the town. The community town, gas station, store, post office and such were abandoned after WWII. The first Postman appointed to Trementina was Martin Gurule in April 1901.

Trementina *Camposanto*:   September 1996/ May 2006

Manuel E. Blea July 7 1931; Pvt. 1CL 34 Inf. 7 Div.
Juana Teresa Blea June 12 1912
Santiago Blea 1849 – December 21 1911
Selso Blea May 9 1932; 68 years
Estevan Cordova 1886 – 1934
Federico Cordova March 20 1895 – April 24 1931
Abelino Estrada January 12 1886 – September 7 1976
Amadeo Estrada November 30 1929 – February 6 1939
Esabelita E. Garcia 1933 – 1933
Juan P. Garcia
Gregorita Gonzales 1920 - 1920
Adela Jaramillo Estrada August 29 1910 – September 29 1986
Irene Jaramillo Estrada 1894 - 1928
Jose Estrada 1905 – 1952
Julian Estrada, Sr. January 7 1865 – December 18 1951
Mired Estrada 1941 - 1993
Obed Estrada 1936 - 1951
Martin Gonzales January 30 1896 – August 27 1980
Audina Blea Jaramillo 1858 -1927
Bernabe Jaramillo October 17 1917 – June 21 1991
Jose Jaramillo 1888 - 1927
Louis "Leo" Jaramillo 1914 - 1931
Martin Jaramillo June 24___ - February ____
Norberto Jaramillo 1846 - 1938

Norma Jaramillo March 20 1942 – April 16 1992
Conferina E. Nieto May 21 1921 – May 11 1991
Gregorita Valverde Gonzales September 23 1989 – March 16 1989
Jose Cicilio Valverde December 5 1866 – February 10 1933

Trementina Creek *Camposanto*: Taken 1993

Diego Aragon   March 25 „97
Josefita Aragon   September 19 1900
Maria Yrinea Blea de Vialpando   November 21 1901
Antonio Griego   November 3 1896
R. Dominguez   June 7 "98 – January 11 „99
Ysabel Garcia   March 20 1895 – January 31 1899
S. G. & G. G.   1898
Camilia Garcia y E   July 18 – September 6 1901
Jose Domingo Cristobal Garcia, d. January 1901, age 76
Maria Antonia Rosa Gonzales   1900
Lusiano Gonzales   March 23 1902
G. S. L.   No. 25 1898
Maria Josefa Madril   December 17 1897
Carlota Martines de G.   July 31 1899
Ramonsita Martines y V.   July 6 1903
Eutimio Padilla   February 12 1902
Bitalia Romero   October 7 1873 – July 31 1903
Jose Antonio Vialpando   November 27 1894
Julia   1887/9

Very few of these headstones are legible or there today.

Trementina, Presbyterian Community Church, La Paz, 1956.
Sara Blea Gonzales and her brother Adolfo Blea, young girl is Sara's granddaughter.
Courtesy of Rubel Margarito Gonzales.

Brands for some near Trementina

Chaperito N.M.
July 25 — 1889

The session met to day, at the close of public service. Members present J. M. Whitlock, and Rafael Rodrigues (the latter elder of the Buena Vista Church) and Rev. James Fraser moderator. The session was opened with prayer. The following persons were examined very carefully and received into the church.

Tomas Gallegos
Manuel Apodaca
Juana Gallegos
Guadalupe Lucero
Aurelia Mestas
Barbara Duran
Maria M. Gallegos
Maria M. Apodaca
Sarita Gallegos
Demacia Mestas
Delphino Gallegos
Maria Gallegos
Miguelita Gallegos

Received at the same time from Los Valles

Jose Blea
Maria J. Blea
Maria D. Blea

The meeting was closed with prayer.

James Fraser
Moderator

July 25, 1889 Converting to Presbyterian -- done at Chaperito and Los Valles.

Maps

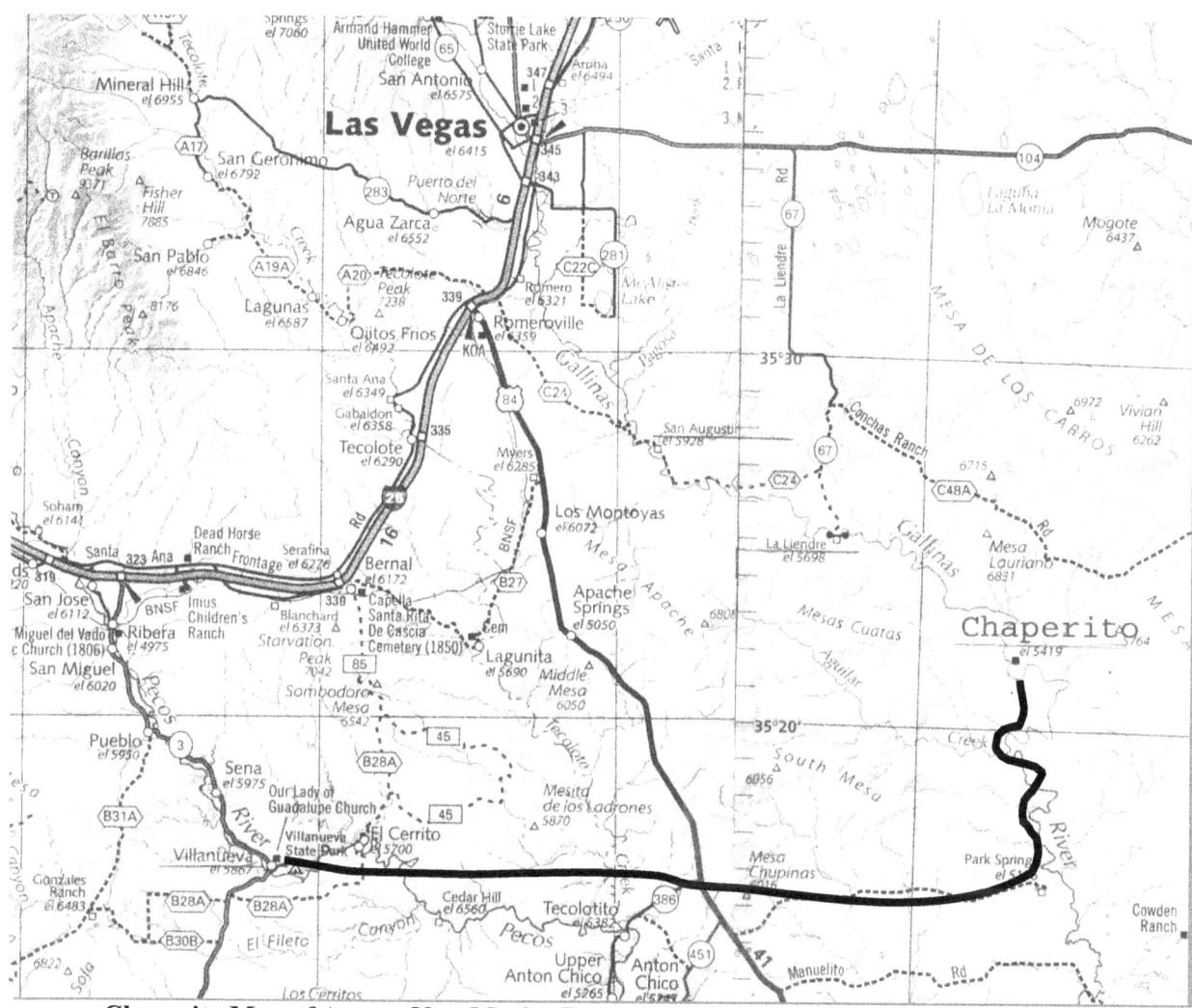

**Chaperito Map of Area —New Mexico Road & Recreation Atlas‖, Pgs. 34-35;
Migration from La Cuesta to Chaperito.**

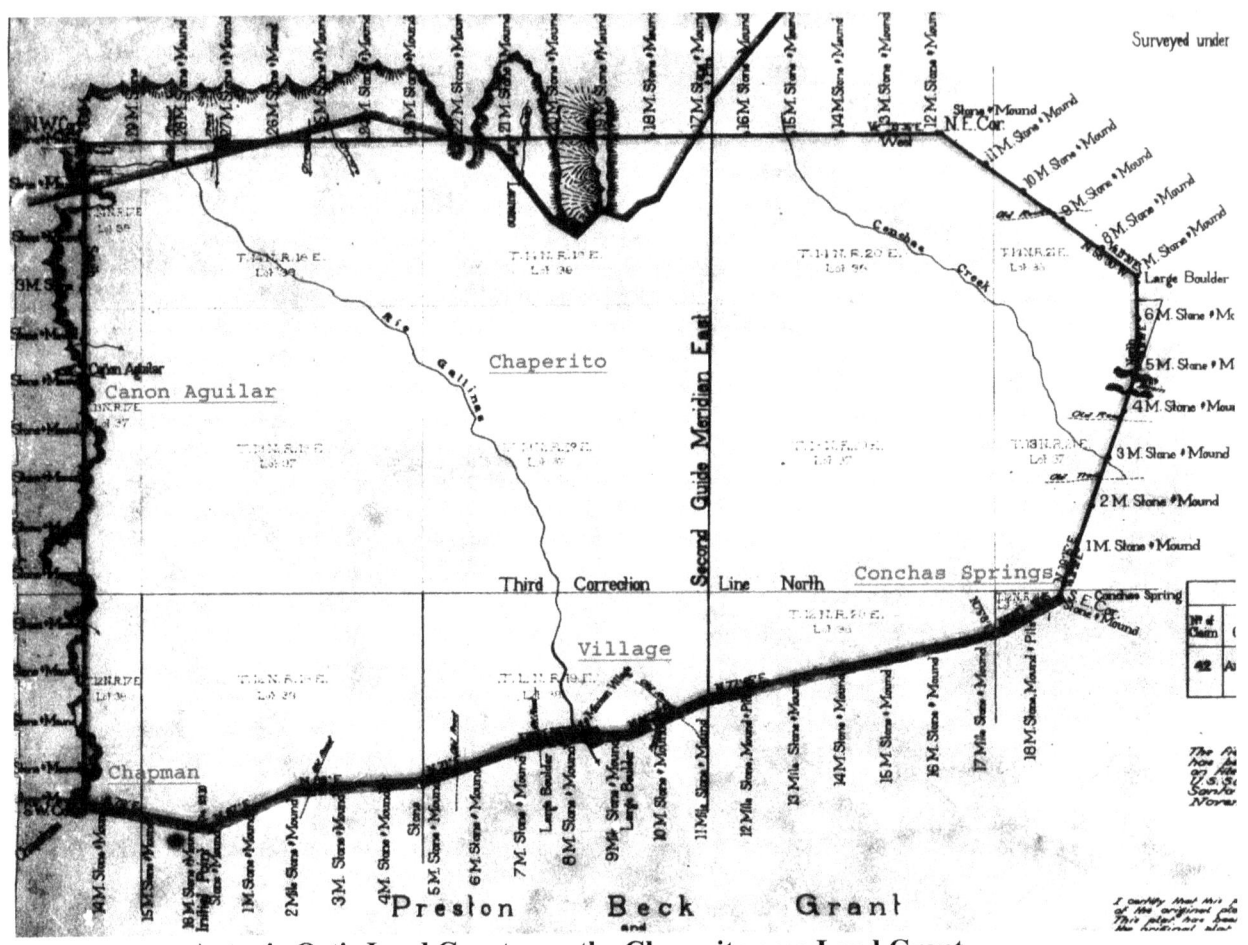

**Antonio Ortiz Land Grant over the Chaperito area Land Grant
BLM Surveyor's Documents**

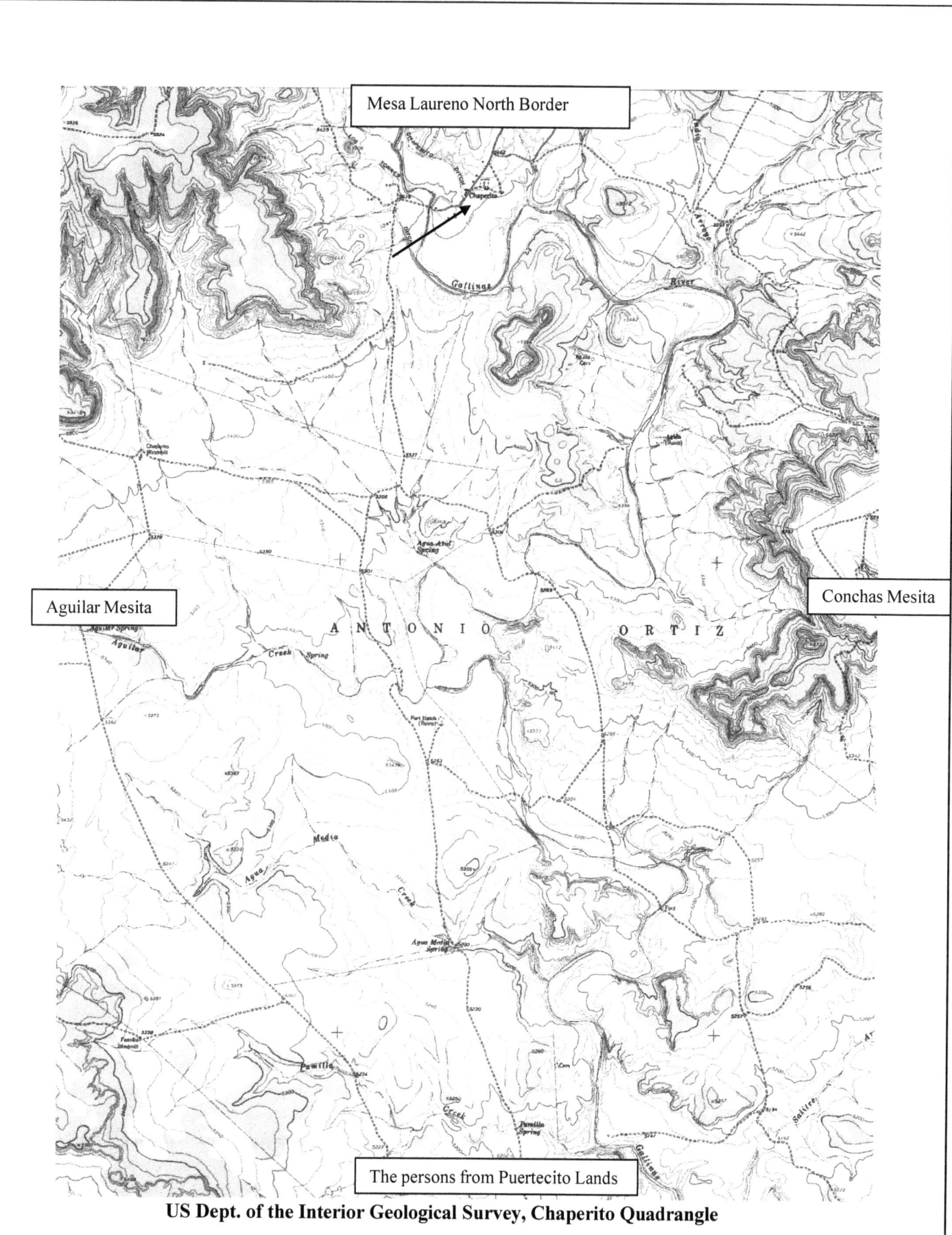

US Dept. of the Interior Geological Survey, Chaperito Quadrangle

Bibliography

Barber, Ruth K., Edith J. Agnew. *Sowers Went Forth.* Menaul Historical Library, 1981.

Cabeza de Baca, Fabiola. *"We Fed Them Cactus"* University of New Mexico Press, 1994.

Christmas, Henrietta M., Ernestino Tafoya & Ruby Olguin. *"New Mexico Census, 1790, 1793, 1803, 1823, 1829, 1841,"* Hispanic Genealogical Research Center of New Mexico, 2009.

Cobos, Ruben. *"A Dictionary of New Mexico & Southern Colorado Spanish,"* Museum of New Mexico Press, 2003.

Ebright, Malcolm. *"Land Grants & Lawsuits in Northern New Mexico,"* University of New Mexico Press, 1994.

Gonzales, Samuel Leo. *"The Days of Old,"* private printing, 1993.

Gregg, Josiah. *"Commerce of the Prairies,"* University of Oklahoma Press, 1954.

Griego, Alfonso. *"Good-bye My Land of Enchantment,"* private printing, 1981.

Hanks, Nancy. *Lamy's Legion, Serving the Archdiocese of Santa Fe from 1850 to 1912.* HRM Books, 2000.

Kavanagh, Thomas W. *"The Comanches, A History 1706-1875".* University of Nebraska Press, 1996.

Morris, John Miller. *"El Llano Estacado: Exploration and Imagination of the High Plains of Texas and New Mexico 1536-1860."* Texas state Historical Association, 1997.

New Mexico Genealogy Society. *"The Genealogist,"* 1983, 1993, 1994, 1997 journals.

Nostrand, Richard L. *"El Cerrito, New Mexico, Eight Generations in a Spanish Village."* University of Oklahoma Press, 2003.

Rathbun, Daniel C. B. & David V. Alexander. *"New Mexico Frontier Military Place Names,"* Yucca Tree Press, 2003.

Rae, Steven R., Joseph E. King, Donald Abbe. *"Historic Bridge Survey for the New Mexico State Highway Department."* May 1984

San Miguel County Clerk"s Office, Deed Books. Las Vegas, NM.

Spanish Archives of New Mexico, Series I, New Mexico State Records Center & Archives, Santa Fe, NM, Roll 30, Chaperito Land Grant

Simmons, Marc. *"Settlement Patterns and Village Plans in Colonial New Mexico."* Reprinted from Journal of the Southwest, Volume VIII, No. 1, January 1969.

Terrell, John Upton. *"The Plains Apache,"* Thomas Y. Crowell Company, New York, 1975.

Thompson, Jerry D. *"New Mexico Territory During the Civil War, Wallen and Evans Inspection Reports, 1862-1863,"* University of New Mexico Press, 2008.

U. S. Federal Census, 1860, 1870, 1880, 1900, San Miguel County, Territory of New Mexico.

INDEX

Cemeteries and musters not indexed.

A

Alarcon , Antonio, 8
Anallo, Francisco, 8
Angel, Eugolio, 38
Angel, Maria Leonara, 38
Angel, Remejio, 8
Anton Chico, 5, 19, 20, 30, 31, 35, 38, 40, 42, 43, 46
Antonio Ortiz Grant, 5, 6, 7
Antonio Ortiz Land Grant, 43, 70
Apodaca , Manuel, 11
Apodaca, Albino, 9
Apodaca, Desiderio, 8
Apodaca, Jose, 8
Apodaca, Jose Crespin, 40
Apodaca, Jose de la Crus, 8
Apodaca, Jose E., 18
Apodaca, Jose Marilla, 9
Apodaca, Jose Miguel, 8, 10, 11, 32
Apodaca, Juan, 8, 36
Apodaca, Labrado, 9
Apodaca, Manuel, 9, 11
Apodaca, Manuel Esquipula, 40
Apodaca, Placido, 7, 8, 27, 35
Apodaca, Trinidad, 8
Aragon, Domingo, 10
Aragon, Esteban, 8
Aragon, Lorenzo, 3
Aragon, Pedro, 8, 27
Aragon, Ygnacio, 3
Archuleta, Jose Miguel, 8
Archuleta, Silverio, 9
Archuleta. Mariano, 9
Arellanes, Florencio, 18
Arellanes, Francisco, 25
Arguello, Juan A., 9
Arguello, Sencion, 9
Arkansas, 26
Armijo, Jose, 3
Armijo, Manuel, 24

B

Baca y Terrus, Jose Francisco, 4
Baca, Amado, 9
Baca, Gabriel, 4
Baca, Jose Benito, 7, 9
Baca, Juan, 4
Baca, Luis, 8
Baca, Manuel, 35
Baca, Miguel, 9
Baca, Ramon, 9
Balland, 22
Balverde, Manuel, 10
Baros, Antonio, 9
Baros, Francisco, 8
Baros, Jose Maria, 9
Baros, Marselino, 9
Belarde, Jose de los Relles, 9
Bell Ranch, 49
Blake, Alice, 20, 24, 42
Blea, Gerorgo, 9
Blea, Juan Francisco, 10
Blea, Lugardo, 3
Blea, Romulo, 42
Blea, Santiago, 18, 32, 42, 65
Bourdier, 19, 22
Bowman, 25
buffalo, 7, 14
buffalo hunters, 1, 6, 65
Butieres, Simon, 8
Butierres, Jose Domingo, 8

C

C de Baca, Ezequiel, 24, 35
Cabra Springs, 30, 49, 65
Cañada de Aguilar, 6, 13, 24, 30, 43
Cañon Largo, 22, 27, 48, 58
Carpentier, 22
Casias, Jose de la Cruz, 11
Chaperito, 1, 2, 3, 4, 5, 6, 7, 8, 10, 12, 13, 14, 15, 18, 19, 20, 21, 22, 23, 24, 25, 26, 27, 30, 31, 35, 38, 40, 42, 43,

45, 46, 47, 48, 49, 50, 51, 55, 58, 62, 63, 64, 68, 69, 70, 71, 73
Chaperito Grant, 5, 6
Chapman, John L., 26
Chaves, Francisco S., 46
Chavez, Carmen, 9
Chavez, Dimas, 9
Chavez, Julio, 9
Chavez, Leo, 24
Cherisco, 64
Chupaines, 6, 7, 30
Ciboleros, 14
Comancheros, 61
Conchas, 3, 4, 6, 7, 13, 19, 22, 26, 46, 49, 55, 62, 63, 64, 65

D

Delavelle, 22
Delgado, Cirilio, 35
Delgado, Sostenes, 25
DeVriesas, 64
Duran, Apolonio, 8
Duran, Atanacio, 8
Duran, Bibion, 10
Duran, Eduardo, 25
Duran, Hilario, 9
Duran, Jose, 4, 10
Duran, Jose de Jesus, 9
Duran, Luis, 8
Duran, Manuela, 38
Duran, Marcos, 9
Duran, Maria de los Remedios, 38
Duran, Matias, 35
Duran, Ramon, 10

E

El Aguila, 13, 18, 20, 30, 42
El Aguilar, 6
El Cerrito, 30, 32
El Cerro, 64
El Choro, 64
El Mesteño, 64
El Salitre, 30
El Tecolotito, 30
Encinias, Antonio, 8
Estrada, Jose Lauriano, 55, 57
Estrada, Maria Luz, 37

F

Flores y Esquibel, Manuel, 8
Flores, Daniel, 9
Flores, Emilio, 9
Flores, Gregorio, 9, 24
Flores, Jose, 8
Flores, Juan, 8
Flores, Leonides, 8
Flores, Manuel, 8, 9, 27
Florez, 25
Fort Bascom, 6, 7
Fort Smith, 26
Fort Sumner, 26
Frouville, 23, 24
Fruville, 23, 25
Ft. Hatch, 1

G

Gallegos, Camilo, 9
Gallegos, Candelario, 8, 27
Gallegos, Cruz, 9
Gallegos, Dolores, 18
Gallegos, Esquipula, 8
Gallegos, Esteban, 8
Gallegos, Francisco, 8, 9
Gallegos, Jesus, 9
Gallegos, Jesus Maria, 24
Gallegos, Jose, 8
Gallegos, Juan Jose, 9
Gallegos, Merejildo, 9
Gallegos, Onofre, 9
Gallegos, Pedro, 11
Gallegos, Ricardo, 8, 11, 28
Gallegos, Tomas, 8
Gallinas River, 3, 4, 5, 6, 10, 17, 26, 31, 38, 40, 42, 45
Gallinas Spring, 45
Galon, 19, 22
Garcia Jose, 4
Garcia y Gonzales, Francisco, 8
Garcia y Urioste, Rafael, 8
Garcia, Andres, 6, 9
Garcia, Atanacio, 9
Garcia, Erculano, 24

Garcia, Felix, 8
Garcia, Herculano, 25
Garcia, Jose, 3, 5, 8, 10
Garcia, Jose Pablo, 24
Garcia, Juan, 10
Garcia, Julian, 3
Garcia, Juliana, 9
Garcia, Lorenzo, 9
Garcia, Miguel, 8, 10, 32
Garcia, Nasario, 9
Garcia, Sencion, 8
Garcia, Simon, 5
Garcia, Teodoro, 9
Garcia, Tiburcio, 8
Garduño, Adolfo C., 25
Garduño, Esperidon, 8
Garduño, Gregorio, 8
Garsia y Carillo, Rafael, 8
Garsilla, Jose Lion, 9
Garsilla, Marcos, 9
Garsilla, Ponsio, 8
Gilberton, 22
Goldsmith, 25
Gomez, Ana Maria, 36, 37
Gomez, Jesus, 8
Gomez, Lucrecio, 8
Gomez, Pablo, 8
Gonsales, Leonordo, 9
Gonsales, Jose de la Cruz, 9
Gonsales, Neposeno, 10
Gonsales, Pablo, 9
Gonzales, Miguel, 27
Gonzales y Apodaca, Francisco, 9
Gonzales y Esquibel, Rafael, 9
Gonzales y Sena, Juan, 9
Gonzales, Antonio, 47
Gonzales, Gabriel, 4, 8, 27
Gonzales, Graviel, 5, 10
Gonzales, Hilaria, 48
Gonzales, Jesus, 4, 5, 10, 11
Gonzales, Manuelita V. de, 47
Gonzales, Marcos, 32
Gonzales, Maria Antonia, 10, 37
Gonzales, Maria Guadalupe, 20
Gonzales, Matias, 8, 27
Gonzales, Miguel Albino, 32

Gonzales, Patrisio, 24
Gonzales, Santiago, 8, 11
Gonzales, Simon, 9
Gonzales, Ygnazio, 8
Gonzalez, Manuel, 25
Gourcy, 22
Gunst, 25
Gurule, Martin, 65

H

Hatch, Alexander, 26
Hatch"s Ranch, 3, 26, 30
Herrera, Encarnacion de, 8
Herrera, Francisco, 11
Herrera, Sefirino de, 9
Hommell, Louis, 24
Hommell, Luis, 24

J

Jacales, 23
Jaramillo, Antonio, 8
Jaramillo, Luis, 8
Jaramillo, Norberto, 42
Jaramillo, Pablo, 8
Jaramillo, Serafina, 40
Jaramillo, Ventura, 8
Jorupa, 30, 40

K

Kueppers, 22

L

La Aguila, 6, 14, 18, 42, 45
La Concepcion, 18, 30, 40
La Cuesta, 1, 3, 4, 5, 6, 17, 30, 69
La Cueva, 30
La Garita, 50, 63
La Liendre, 6, 13, 19, 20, 23, 24, 30, 35, 36, 40, 43
Lamy, 19, 31, 35, 40
Las Conchas, 6, 62
Las Lajas, 6, 13, 38
Las Vegas, 1, 3, 4, 5, 6, 10, 17, 19, 23, 25, 26, 27, 31, 35, 38, 40, 72
Laureno, 6, 7

Leger, Carlota, 40
Leger, Francisco, 31
Leyva, Jose Nestor, 24
llano estacado, 14
Loma de Montosa, 30
Lopes, Juan Acencion, 11
Lopez, Ana Maria, 31
Lopez, Esquipula, 8
Lopez, Jose, 35
Lopezville, 46
Los Alamitos, 64
Los Alamosas, 64
Los Esteritos, 30
Los Fuertes, 30, 32, 38, 39, 65
Los Lajas, 30
Los Luceros, 13, 30, 42
Los Torres, 5, 6, 11, 13, 22, 30, 38
Los Valles de San Agustin, 3, 10, 19, 20, 27, 31
Los Valles de San Antonio, 35
Lovato, Jose, 8
Lower Las Gallinas, 30
Lucero, Antonio Maria, 8
Lucero, Canuto, 9
Lucero, Dolores, 9
Lucero, Eusebio, 8
Lucero, Felipe M., 9
Lucero, Fernando, 3, 10
Lucero, Francisco, 9
Lucero, Higinio, 9
Lucero, Jose, 9, 10, 25
Lucero, Jose E., 8
Lucero, Jose Nieves, 3
Lucero, Jose Romulo, 9
Lucero, Jose Ynosencio, 9
Lucero, Juan Climaco, 8
Lucero, Juan de la Cruz, 5, 8
Lucero, Lucrecio, 8
Lucero, Pedro, 9
Lucero, Placido, 9
Lucero, Rafael, 3
Lucero, Telesfor, 8
Lucero, Victoriano, 9
Lujan, Ramon, 48
Lusero, Felis, 8
Lusero, Francisco, 19

M

Madrid, Felipe, 4
Madrid, J. Pablo, 31
Madrid, Jose Pablo, 35
Madrid, Juan, 3
Madrid, Pablo, 42
Madril, Jose, 9
Madril, Jose Felipe, 11
Madril, Josefa, 9
Maes, Deciderio, 3
Maes, Juan de Dios, 4, 5, 10, 16
Maes, Manuel, 15
Maes, Maria Ramona, 16
Maestas, Filomeno, 9
Maestas, Necolas, 42
Maldonado, Pedro, 10
Mangas, 64
Mares, Maria Rita, 9
Margarita Muñiz, 43
Marques, Pedro, 31
Marquez, Manuel, 24
Marquez, Rafael, 4
Marquez, Rebecca, 37
Martin Santiago, 4
Martin, Desiderio, 35
Martin, Salbador, 8
Martin, Santiago, 3
Martines, Abraham, 19
Martines, Gabriel, 8
Martines, Jesus, 8, 28
Martines, Jose Leon, 24
Martines, Juan, 9
Martines, Juan de, 9
Martines, Nicolas, 8, 11, 28
Martinez , Hurbano, 35
Martinez , Jose Domingo, 37
Martinez, Anacleto, 10
Martinez, Carlos, 25, 40
Martinez, Jesus M., 25
Martinez, Jose Leon, 35
Martinez, Ramon, 18
Martinez, Santiago, 7
Martinez, Sixto, 50
Martino, Carmel, 9
Mayeux, 22
Mendosa, Rafael, 10

Mestas, Maria Dolores, 38
Mestas, Nicolas, 8, 11, 27
Miguel Albino Gonzales, 27
Montaño, 10, 11, 28
Montaño, Juan Pedro, 9
Montaño, Luis S., 9
Montaño, Patricio, 9
Montoya y Martinez, Manuel, 7
Montoya, Benigno, 9
Montoya, Manuel, 8, 19, 27
Mora, 48
Mora, Juan, 8
Mt. Pleasant, 30
Mtz., Jose Guadalupe, 10
Muñiz, 11
Muñiz, Jesus, 43

N

Nolan, Lola, 61
Norias, 64

O

Ojo de Las Gallinas, 45
Olgin, Francisco, 11
Olgin, Pablo, 4
Olguin, Francisco, 10
Ortega, Eligio, 9
Ortega, Pablo, 9
Ortiz Grant. *See* Antonio Ortiz Grant
Ortiz, Tomas, 5

P

Pacheco, Tomas, 9
Padia, Rafael, 31
Padia, Zenon, 31
Pinon, Ynes, 9
Plantard, 22
Puertecito, 3, 4

R

Rael, Jose, 3
Rael, Juan, 10, 11, 38
Rael, Maria Petra, 38
Ramirez, Maria Apolonia, 51
Ribera, Maria Dolores, 38

Ribera, Pedro, 9
Rincon de los Chupaines, 6
Rio Colorado, 49
Rivera, Jose Gregorio, 9
Rivera, Pablo, 8, 28
Robledo, 6, 25
Robledo, Francisco E., 6, 8, 25
Rociada, 48, 51, 61
Romero, Antonio A., 9
Romero, Jose, 9
Romero, Trinidad, 6
Roybal, Cecilio, 16
Ruibal, Antonio D., 9
Ruibal, Francisco, 9
Ruiz, Gonzalo, 24

S

Sabino, 64
Sabinoso, 13, 18, 23, 24, 30, 48, 64
Sais, Miguel Ramon, 3
Sais, Tomas, 3
Salas, Francisco, 3, 6
Salas, Ramon, 9
Salas, Teodosio, 6
Salas, Tiodoso, 9
Salazar, Abran, 42
Salazar, Antonio, 8
Salitre, 65
San Agustin, 13, 29, 30, 31, 32, 33
San Augustin, 31, 32, 65
San Hilario, 50, 63
San Lorenzo, 20, 22, 23, 24, 30, 46
San Miguel del Bado, 5, 10, 19, 32, 35,
    37, 38, 43, 45, 48
San Ramon, 59, 60, 64
Sanchez, Antonio, 61
Sanchez, Jesus Maria, 35
Sanchez, Manuel A., 61
Sanchez, Rafael, 51
Sandobal, Teodoro, 9
Sandoval, Abran, 9
Sena, Antonio, 9
Sena, Francisco, 9
Sena, Higinio, 9
Sena, Jose Ynes, 9
Sena, Juan, 8

Sheep, 17, 18
Sisneros, Maria Nieves, 37
Splinters, 22
Straus, 25

T

Tafoya, Isidro, 18
Tafoya, Teofilo, 42
Tafoya, Ysidro, 9
Tapia, Felipe, 35
Tapia, Guadalupe, 8
Tapia, Jose, 3, 10
Tapia, Jose Antonio, 3
Tapia, Jose Manuel, 3, 6, 10
Tapia, Juan Jesus, 8
Tapia, Maria del Refugio, 43
Tapia, Mauricio, 15
Tapia, Prudencio, 3
Tapia, Salvador, 37
Tapia, Severo, 24, 43
Taylor Ranch, 30
Torres, Maria Sista, 38
Torres, Refugio, 28, 38

Trementina, 13, 17, 18, 22, 24, 30, 32, 42, 46, 51, 55, 59, 61, 62, 64, 65, 66, 67
Trujeque, Jose Miguel, 20
Trujillo, Isidoro, 24
Tucumcari, 64

U

Ulibarri, Felix, 26

V

Valdez, Encarnacion, 8
Valdez, Lorenzo, 19
Valverde, Cecilio, 42
Valverde, Macedon, 38
Valverde, Teodora, 38
Variadero, 22, 50, 55, 56, 57, 62
Velasquez, Tomas, 8
Vigil, Presentasion D., 24
Vigil, Santos, 9

Y

Ygnacio Aragon, 11

www.ingramcontent.com/pod-product-compliance
Lightning Source LLC
Chambersburg PA
CBHW080349170426
43194CB00014B/2731